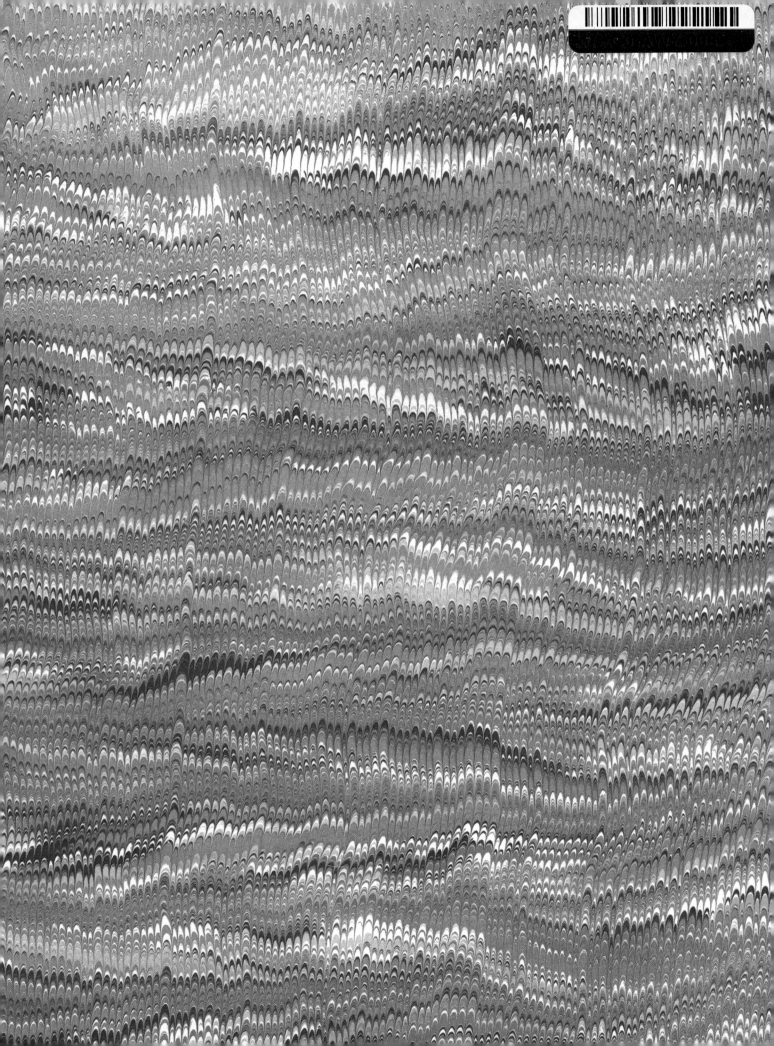

# American

# Factory Decoys

by

Henry A. Fleckenstein, Jr.

*Schiffer Publishing Ltd*

*Box E, Exton, Pennsylvania 19341*

# Acknowledgements

Many thanks go out to many people without whose help and cooperation this book would never have been done. I would particularly like to thank my wife Barbara, for all she has had to put up with during the work on the research and writing, and for all of the typing and proof reading which was her job alone. Personal thanks go to Morty and Carol Kramer and Dan and Maggie Brown for opening their homes and collections of factory decoys to me, and to an especially fine friend, Michael Luby, for all of his help and interest in the project.

Equally important for their contributions were the following people and organizations - Roger Ludwig, Hugh Valiant, Joe French, Joe Crockett, George Boen, Dick Lancaster, Dave Johnson, Tom Witte, Dick Clark, Bobby Richardson, Arthur Birdsall, Chris Nelson, Charles Frank, Hal Sorenson, Peter Muller, Ed Spevak, Dale Horst, Sam Dyke, Ron Gard, Bob Horner, Bill Butler, Les Brown, Bill Underwood, Otto Johs, Doug McConnell, Ken Callahan of Callahan & Co. Books in Easton, Dave Morrison, Dick McIntyre, Rick Brown, John Sullivan, Ron Kurzman, Joe Johnson, the Jackson Family, Ted Harmon, Shelburne Museum, The Museums at Stony Brook, Refuge Waterfowl Museum, Decoy Collectors Guide of Burlington, Iowa, and the Folklife Departments of the Smithsonian Institution, Bob Michelson, Bob Jones, Jim and Joan Siebert, and for any whose name I've missed, thank you and please forgive me for missing your name.

*Layout and Design: Steve Carothers*

Copyright © 1981 Henry A. Fleckenstein, Jr.

Library of Congress catalog card number: 81-51446

ISBN: 0-916838-52-8

This book may be ordered directly from Schiffer Publishing, Box E, Exton, PA 19341. Please include $1.50 postage in U.S.A. Please try your local book store first.

Printed in the United States of America.

# Dedication

FOR MOM AND DAD —
          WHO RAISED ME TO AN OUTDOORS ETHIC.

*A Wildfowler black duck rig still being used - at
"the shore." (Collection of the author.)*

*A pile of decoys that includes at least one example of most of the factories or commercial makers that are covered in this book. (Collection of the author.)*

# Table of Contents

*A rig of Victor Animal Trap Company divers with a
lone widgeon.*

# Introduction

# "Factory Decoys"

Duck decoys have been used by hunters in the United States to lure wildfowl to their guns since the time of the American Revolution, and during the last two hundred years many gunners have made their own decoys in a manner to suit their particular circumstances of hunting. Every hunter had his own idea of what would constitute the perfect decoy, one that would be effective in tolling the birds, easy to carry and rig out, and relatively inexpensive and simple to make. Through long hard years of hunting experience and the uninterrupted, profound thought that can occur on a slow day in a duck blind, he would develop the ideas that would ultimately result in that elusive, just right decoy.

For the first hundred years the wooden blocks employed by the hunter were entirely made and painted by hand, that is, the maker used hand tools such as the hatchet, drawknife, whittling knife, and wood rasp to form his birds. He started with a simple block of white pine or cedar and fashioned, through the use of these hand tools, a respectably appropriate representation of a live duck. Finished with paint in the pattern of the real bird, it served his purpose well when on the water and in many cases provided the outlet for the creative talent which lays dormant in most men. Whether the shooter was a market hunter, a local bayman hunting to provide food for his family, or in later years, the sport hunter, these hand made decoys were used exclusively until the gunning for market and for sport blossomed into a prominent activity in the 1870's

and the demand for decoys noticeably increased. To be sure many decoy makers were probably commercially making and selling decoys before this time, particularly in areas of heavy gunning such as the Susquehanna Flats, but the need for decoys accelerated rapidly during this period to the point that inventive minds began looking for quicker, easier methods for producing decoys.

Some of the innovative, would be inventors came up with rather unusual ideas employing materials heretofore unheard of for decoys; examples such as the hollow tin folding shore birds patented in 1874 in Boston and made by a number of different companies into the 1920's. These decoys were made in halves, hollow stamped out of tin, and then fastened with wire hinges so that they would open and nest inside one another for storage and easy transporting. They would then form a full bodied bird when folded into the closed position. There was the hollow tin decoy with a wooden body board equipped with a battery driven propeller designed so that it would swim around in the water among the other decoys. A number of other hollow stamped tin or sheet metal decoys were produced including one named the Brinkop Metal Decoy that was advertised in the 1894-95 Montgomery Ward catalog. The author has in his collection a most unusual unknown ruddy duck with a wooden lathe turned body and a hollow tin head. It was discovered in North Carolina by Vernon Berg and was purchased from his collection.

Several decoy companies in the mid-west

7

and west manufactured decoys that were made of sewn canvas, waterproofed and printed with elaborate feather patterns, and filled with excelsior or kapok. These birds must have served the waterfowl hunter well as quite a number of them turn up today; they make very interesting additions to any collection of decoys.

Other commercial decoy enterprises were just as fanciful and creative such as the decoy patented in 1888 with sheet metal wings that flapped when pulled by a string running back to the blind, and the flying decoys by the Tuveson Company that had wooden bodies with canvas outspread wings attached. They were mounted on a stake out in the water or allowed to slide down a taut cable stretched from the blind down toward the other decoys placed in front of the hide. Another departure from the ordinary, a rather novel idea, was a cork decoy with a quacking mechanism inside that was activated by squeezing a bulb on the end of a long rubber tube that ran back to wherever the gunner was hidden.

The imaginative mind that was inspired by this notion apparently believed in his creation as it was patented and advertised in several national sporting magazines. Unfortunately records of its effectiveness are not known. There were scores of different ideas similar to these that included decoys that swam, made noises, bobbed their heads, flapped, dipped under water, and flew and were made of cork, paper mache, tin, sheet metal, canvas, straw, cotton, and early plastics and rubber. In the book *American Wild-Fowl Shooting* written by Joseph W. Long and published in New York in 1874, a section on decoys mentions the would-be inventors who made decoys of rubber, tin, and copper. Mr. Long's writing goes on to make it very plain that none of these early inventions could compare to the early hand carved wooden decoys.

There also were factory or commercial decoys made of wood and the earliest examples seem to have been made of this oldest of decoy making materials. Decoys that were commercially made entirely by hand, but today are considered factory decoys by collectors, appeared during the 1860's. Harvey Stevens of Weedsport, New York turned out the finest of these by hand with beautifully applied paint patterns and today they are sought avidly by many collectors. An unusually exciting American widgeon decoy by Stevens was sold at Bourne Auction in 1980 for the sum of $3900, the highest price paid yet for a Stevens bird.

Early wooden decoys that were turned on a lathe and can truly qualify as factory made decoys surfaced ten years later during the 1870's. Earliest among these seems to be an M. C. Wedd from Rochester, New York who advertised in *Forest and Stream Magazine* during the 1870's. A very early common merganser decoy by the Wedd Company is pictured in Plate 143 in William Mackey's book *American Bird Decoys*. To date that is the only bird thought to have been made by this New York company that is known, and little or no further information has surfaced.

From the 1890's through the 1940's, commercially made factory decoys flourished and were manufactured by the thousands until the duck shooting began to decline and with it the need for large quantities of decoys. Some of the better known companies such as Mason Decoy Company, Evans Decoys, Hays Decoy Company, Pratt Decoys, and Wildfowler Decoys produced birds that are very collectable today and are as eagerly pursued as any of the classic hand made decoys which fill collectors shelves.

William J. Mason began his decoy making business in 1896 in Detroit, Michigan. Within five to seven years his young company had grown into quite an enterprise and employed a number of workers producing a quality lathe turned, but hand finished decoy. The birds were offered in several different grades, even though each was made to a rather simple pattern that exhibited little or no carving and was not what one would refer to as fancy. His story of success probably came about in big part because of the beautiful paint patterns that were applied by hand by a number of artistically inclined workers in his factory. The finished decoy was sturdy, functional and presented a realistic appearance on the water. This accounts for the fact that they were popular among hunters and were shipped to all parts of this country. Their durable, appealing paint work that has survived so well until today is the primary factor for their extreme desirability and value to collectors at present. At the annual decoy auction in Hyannis, Massachusetts in July 1980, a pair of Mason mergansers or sheldrakes as they are called in the Mason catalogs, sold for the record price of $5800 for the pair. A similar pair had sold at auction in 1975 in New York City for $2400 for the pair. Undoubtably, Mason decoys are among the most popular of factory decoys among the collectors today.

The Evans Decoy Company was started by Walter Evans of Ladysmith, Wisconsin in the early 1920's. Evans made fine sturdy decoys in three grades - mammoth, standard, and competitive - and in 1931 they sold by the dozen for $20.00, $12.50, and $10.00 respectively. They were well painted with white lead mixed with base colors in the pattern of canvasback, bluebill, redhead, mallard, pintail, teal, and coot. Made of well seasoned local white cedar, they have survived until today in fine fashion to take their place in the decoy collector's world.

Decoys by the J. M. Hays Wood Products Company resemble closely the style and paint patterns of the Mason decoys and for years confused collectors who thought they had Masons, but just weren't quite sure. The company was located in Jefferson City, Missouri and offered decoys for many species in the "Grand Prix," their top of the line model and the "Superior," their second grade. Hays offered their own lead keels with the company name and city impressed into the lead on each side of a key. They offered the keel weight inset flush into the bottom of the decoy and finding a decoy with this keel intact provides positive identification. Hays stated in their ads and catalog that they raised wild ducks on their own private five acre lake so that they could more accurately shape and paint their decoys "true to life." After studying the Hays product and the Mason decoy, one guesses that the Hays factory was more inspired by their Detroit competitor than they were by the live birds on their private lake.

The William E. Pratt Manufacturing Company produced wooden decoys at their Joliet, Illinois manufacturing plant from about 1921 until William Pratt died in 1939. The birds were turned out on reproducing lathes and finished smooth for their higher grade models. The feather finish merely meant leaving the circular lathe marks on the decoys unsanded. They were hand painted very nicely in earlier years and later, for matters of expediency, were spray painted. The Pratt Company during its peak years could turn out as many as ninety dozen decoys a day and many thousands of these birds were sold through Montgomery Ward and Sears Roebuck during the twenties and thirties for $10.00 a dozen. Until recent years, the Pratt decoys were worth only a little more than their original price to decoy collectors. Now many collectors, new and old, are interested in adding an unusual or mint condition Pratt to their collections. When William Pratt died in 1939, the company was sold to the Animal Trap Company of Lititz, Pennsylvania.

The Wildfowler Decoy Company started its long history in the business of manufacturing decoys in 1939 under the able leadership of Edward Mulliken in Old Saybrook, Connecticut, and after being sold three times to new owners is still in production today in Babylon, New York. The present owners are Amel and Karen Massa. They purchased the company and name from Charles Birdsall of Point Pleasant, New Jersey, who in turn bought it from Robert H. Standiford of Quogue, New York. Thus, the line of production has remained unbroken since 1939 and quality decoys have been made by the Wildfowler Decoy Company for forty-three years.

Decoys by a number of other companies, equally well known, but whose product is just beginning to generate interest among collectors will also be covered in this book. The Animal Trap Company of Lititz,

Pennsylvania has a long and important history of producing waterfowl decoys under their trademark "VICTOR" at their decoy manufacturing plant in Pascagoula, Mississippi. From their wooden decoys first made in 1939 to the paper mache decoys of the late 1940's and early 1950's, they have made a significant contribution to the history of wildfowling and decoy making. The Victor decoy is rightfully receiving the appreciation of collectors today that it deserves. Decoys Unlimited of Erie, Pennsylvania made very fine oversize hunting decoys in most species found along the Atlantic Flyway. All of their decoys had better than average paint patterns with intricate comb and scratch feathering. They are found in the collections of those interested in the different makes of factory decoys. J. W. Reynolds of Forest Park, Illinois made at least three different models of decoys during the time the company was in business. Their first offering was the collapsible printed cotton bird that folded down flat on the wooden base to which it was attached. The design was probably influenced by the Acme Folding Decoy Company which produced a very similar decoy at a much earlier date. Reynolds later offered a folding silhouette V-board with three birds, usually two drakes and a hen. It was spring loaded and had very fine durable paint patterns applied. Again the style was very similar to an earlier decoy V-board produced by J. Coudon and Co. of Aikin, Maryland. The painting on the Coudon silhouettes was a sharp departure from the patterns used by the decoy makers in the local area, but compared more to the paint on the better factory birds produced in the mid-west. The Reynolds paint was much the same as the decoys made and painted along the Illinois River. J. W. Reynolds also produced wooden full bodied, lathe turned birds almost identical in style to the lower grade Pratt decoys, except that the painting, again, was very well done and professional in appearance. A pair of original condition pintails were sold in session IV of the William Mackey sale at the Bourne Auction Galleries in 1973. Eight years ago they brought $225.00, so

perhaps we should say that these birds have already been added to the list of collectible decoys by today's standards.

The term "factory decoy" as applied to the title of this book should be made clear at this point so that as one enters the main part of the book he will have some idea of what to expect. Factory decoy, as intended for inclusion in this work will be defined as decoys roughed out on duplication machinery or birds commercially advertised for sale in sporting journals or catalogs. This seems to be the accepted delineation in the decoy collecting world today. Many of these decoys had very much more hand work put into their production than by any machine. The decoys made in Havre de Grace, Maryland from about 1925 until today are a perfect example of this idea. They will not be covered in this book for several reasons. The author collects decoys from the Susquehanna Flats and the Havre de Grace decoys are included in this group. It has long been believed by myself and others who seriously collect these lathe turned decoys that the amount of hand work and hand painting that goes into finishing off the roughed out block as it comes off of the lathe qualifies these birds as other than machine made, with the sometimes lesser connotation that that term proffers. Robert F. McGaw appears to have been the innovator in Havre de Grace who designed and had built a lathe with which he could turn the heavy wood off of a decoy block. His manner was quickly followed by R. Madison Mitchell and Paul Gibson. These two gentlemen are still producing wooden decoys in this manner today in Havre de Grace, although Madison Mitchell recently sold his business to Mr. William Collins. Bill continues to turn out the same fine decoy that Mr. Mitchell produced for some fifty-six years. Latter day understudies to Mr. Mitchell who own their own lathes and make wooden decoys are Captain Harry Jobes and Jimmy Pierce.

The decoys made by these men are initially turned on a duplicating lathe to the approximate size and shape of the finished body. The breast and tail stock that was held on center by the chucks are then cut off and the body is worked down with a draw knife and spoke shave, two early woodworking tools. The body is then sanded and has a hand carved head applied. The entire bird is then patched or filled if needed, sanded some more, and hand painted in a manner that dates back to the early part of this century. It is easy enough to recognize that the birds could as easily be classed as hand made as machine made.

A second reason for their exclusion from this book is that the Havre de Grace decoys and decoy makers will be covered fully in a book by the author on Upper Chesapeake Bay decoys scheduled for publication in the next couple of years. It will be more complete and definitve than anything published to date.

Many of the commercially advertised or factory decoys listed in the alphabetical order in the book will have no more information included than an advertisement from a magazine or a photograph. Research on the part of the author at several libraries, including the Library of Congress, and the Patent Office failed to uncover any additional information. The idea was to include the name or whatever little information was available in the hopes that it might provide someone with a lead, however slight, on a decoy which they may own. In addition any further information on any of the companies listed in this book that would be forwarded to the author will be considered for inclusion in a possible revision of the book.

*A crow shooting rig made by Grayson Chesser of Jenkins Bridge, Virginia. Note the movable wings that flap on the owl decoy. (Collection of the author.)*

# The Crow Shoot

The American crow has always rated a high position on the varmit or pest list of the sportsmen who engage in the fascinating pastime of hunting small game and upland birds. Largely through the influence of this group he has been persecuted not only by the hunter, but also by the farmer and just about every country boy whose imagination was ever captured by the printed media. Much maligned in fact and fiction writing, the crow was always depicted as the bad guy, robbing the eggs and young of our song birds, our quail, pheasants, and grouse and depleting the squirrel and rabbit population by preying on their young. And they most certainly wreak havoc on the marshes and meadows that provide nesting sites for our ducks and geese during their breeding season. Our sporting magazines of the first forty years of this century are filled with advertisements, cartoons, and articles directed toward the decimation of the black hordes of *corvus brachyrhynchos*. The displays implore the sportsmen afield to shoot the crows whenever they are chanced upon while hunting more desirable game, and young boys are urged to practice their plinking with their new .22 rifle on the live target, Mr. Crow, instead of the old reliable stationary tin can. Black connotes bad and the common crow with his coal black feathers has certainly lived up to his reputation, at least in the opinion of many. The crow has been the center of controversy and debate for at least the past eighty years between those who would exterminate it and those who would add it to the list of protected songbirds. Ornithologists long ago discovered that the depredations of this bird on song and game birds and crops is often outweighed by the good it performs in keeping a check on the multitudes of pestiferous insects. Yet in certain areas, controls on the crow population are necessary to hold down their plundering. This is particularly true, as mentioned earlier, in the pothole country of our north central states and Canada where the majority of our waterfowl nest and raise their young.

*American crow decoy by Harry Waite of West Chester, Pennsylvania. (Collection of the author.)*

*Old owl decoy by the Molded Carry-Lite Company. (Collection of the author.)*

The crow shoot is a sport that many of us grew up on, learning our proper leads and distances for a more important time, that of opening day for quail or canvasback. Today crow shooting is regulated by the law and the organized crow shoot for the most part has gone the way of the spring merganser hunt and twenty-five cent gasoline. He was added to the list of protected birds in 1978 under the Crow Act and may be shot out of season only when caught in the act of depredating crops or fowl. Of course the guardians of such laws sometimes look the other way, because they believe, as do many others, that the crow begins depredating when the sun rises in the morning and should be shot on sight. Nevertheless, today the common crow is free to roam safely through most of the year in the United States.

In the time of our youth, however, when the aforementioned list against the crow was added to the fact that they eagerly responded to calls and decoys and the knowledge that prepared properly they could be as tasty as some of our well known gamebirds, one had the ingredients necessary to seriously seek the crow. Now the crow is no pushover, but rather quite clever and wary. If you find that hard to believe, the next time you are in the woods, try sneaking up on one. On the other hand, he is extremely gregarious and likes nothing better than a raucous gathering of his rowdy cohorts to engage in terrorizing an innocent owl unfortunate enough to have been discovered by one of the black ruffians. Should you ever be in your favorite wood lot or field and hear a tremendous clamoring and carrying on by brother crow and his friends, you may safely bet that an owl, hawk, fox, or some other woodland denizen has been espied away from his lair and is being duly harrassed. One crow can raise a racket that will be heard by and will draw every crow within a couple of miles or at least it seems so. They appear as if from nowhere and immediately join in on the fun. Thus the scene is set for the hunter. After reading this, even the novice realizes that all that was needed for a good crow shoot was a call, an owl decoy and several crow decoys.

In days gone by, many farmers directed their assault on the crow because it often took advantage of the open poultry pens to drop in and make off with the young of the domestic fowl. They also believed the crow seriously damaged their grain crops, but in many instances the crows were feeding on the cutworms and other insect pests that were themselves destroying the plantings.

All of this interest in doing away with the common crow developed into a sporting endeavor that continued to excite sportsmen across our country until the shooting of the crow out of season was outlawed.

*Wooden crow decoy once used in Western Virginia. (Collection of the author.)*

A morning of good sport could be had for the expenditure of a few dollars. If one could set up their rig in close proximity to the town dump, then so much the better, because old *corvus*, always curious and hungry, found the local landfill delightfully to his liking.

The author can remember such a time and place, long ago, before rules, regulations, and restrictions were so much a burdensome load on our lives. The place was the old town dump on Tollgate Road just outside of our tiny community of Fallston, with a dirt road leading into it and no fences to keep you out. Up a hill and off to one side was a pit where the refuse was unloaded and periodically burned. Open fields bordered the front of the pit and a cutover wood lot backed up to it. Plenty of cover and lots of food, a perfect set-up for crows. And they always seemed to be there. We took care of our trash at home, but we had often seen the crows at the dump on our travels along our own personal trail to adventure. This path was the old Maryland and Pennsylvania

Railroad tracks and when I think back to my boyhood experiences, many of my brother Charles' and my most exciting encounters were along this railroad's path. Although we lived outside of Fallston proper our trips along the tracks often originated from there, usually from Amrheins store from which we purchased an R.C. Cola and a Moon Pie that were our provisions on our trek. To the south of Fallston lay Henry Wilson's farm, my very first place of employment, where old "Josh" Henry and my friends and I worked with a team of mules until the late 1950's, and made apple cider each fall on an ancient wooden hand operated cider press.

The railroad tracks ran directly through the middle of the antediluvian relict of a farm and immediately thereafter entered Laurel Brook, a paradise that should be within the grasp of every young boy during the heyday of youth. Here were miles of unbroken woods, untouched through the years in some secret spots, traversed in every direction by tumbling, gurgling streams, unspoiled to the taste, clear, cold

*A line up of owl decoys once used for crow shooting. From left: A General Fibre Company owl, a D-7 Victor owl, unknown, another Victor, and a Molded Carry-lite. (Collection of the author.)*

and fresh. All of these tiny rivulets were alive with crawdads, frogs, turtles, snakes and native brook trout, the likes and size of which never ceased to amaze me.

The streams seemingly bounced over the rocks and tree roots down through the hills to empty into each other and then into the Little Gunpowder Falls or Laurel Brook as it was known here; the river from which the entire area received its name. Here deer romped in untold numbers, feeding in the grain fields on its edges, and dropping down wraith like in the still evening to the stream side for a cool drink. The whippoorwills, indefatigably communing with one another, their only companions. Here too, reigned the wood duck and the small mouth bass, both champions of untrampled pure wilderness. To record just one of the countless finer points of this woodland haven that so fascinated me was the fact that seven different species of woodpeckers were commonly seen there. Similar facts of interest to an amatuer naturalist were customary. The railroad tracks crossed over three old wooden

trestles while wending their way through Laurel Brook and I'm not sure if we found more delight in the dangerous exhilaration of treading carefully across the high trestles or fishing for the wary trout and small mouth bass that abounded in the brooks beneath them. The southwestern most trestle crossed the Little Gunpowder River and then perhaps the longest stretch of tangent on the Ma & Pa, as she was affectionately known, carried up past Hidden Pond, endowed with immense large mouth bass. The pond was right next to the railbed, but in the woods and could not be seen from the track, hence our name. Directly next to the track on the other side, atop a steep hill overlooking Laurel Brook, was the largest copperhead den that Charlie and I ever discovered. The Baltimore Zoo was the recipient of a forty-two inch copperhead, the longest they had ever been given, as a result of that uncovering. That tangent stretch was needed for the antiquated road engines to attain the speed needed to tackle the 3.0 percent grade into Fallston that began

*A wooden crow decoy by Harry Shourds of Seaville, New Jersey. (Collection of the author.)*

*An unknown wooden silhouette crow with attached wings from Pennsylvania. (Collection of the author.)*

*A balsa wood crow decoy by Herter's Company of Waseca, Minnesota. (Collection of the Author.)*

*Ad (Courtesy of Field & Stream Magazine. June 1939.)*

*Ad (Courtesy of Outdoor Life Magazine. October 1925.)*

*Ad (Courtesy of Field & Stream Magazine. December 1958.)*

*Ad (Courtesy of Field & Stream Magazine. August 1935.)*

*Ad (Courtesy of Hunting and Fishing Magazine. August 1938.)*

as the railroad crossed the Overshot Brook, one of the trout hideways and Bottom Road which paralleled the stream and to this day remains a dirt road unchanged in thirty years. Many the day that my bicycle was ridden down Friendship Road and into Bottom Road to reach Overshot Trestle and watch old Number 41 hit the end of the tangent and the beginning of the grade in full stride with the morning freight strung out behind her.  Occasionally we were allowed to step on the four wheel bobber tacked on the rear end as the old train groaned over the third and last trestle in Laurel Brook at five miles per hour.  We would talk with the brakeman the short distance into Fallston and then disembark unobtrusively and disappear into Amrheins Store. I am sure the superintendant never realized this sort of thing went on, but it was the very best kind of a railroad.

But pardon me for digressing, the real story lies to the north along the Ma & Pa's tracks. For here, a short distance from Fallston after crossing Winter's Run on yet another trestle, the tortuous curves of the railroad pass by the old dump and here on our walks when we were boys is where we would see the crows. So one day my brother, myself, and several friends decided to take on the black rascals at the dump. The crows were there when we arrived, enjoying their midday snack on top of the heap. As we pulled in they scattered to the woods and sat watching our every move, their desultory calls harshly scolding us for interrupting their meal, but also, it appeared, waiting anxiously to see what new morsels we might leave behind. Three of us got out of the pick-up with our guns and lunch, ducked quickly into some brush near the edge of the garbage heap and hid while my brother Charlie drove out of sight to conceal the truck. After he made his way back through the woods and rejoined us, we settled down to wait for the crows to come back to their feeding and our waiting guns. Cunning were the crows, but not nearly as shrewd and crafty as the hunters who waited for them - or so we thought. We had a long wait. We soon realized that the crows were not going to be as easy as we had imagined. We left that day with one crow amongst the four of us, a foolish bird who came from afar and did not realize that four anxious guns were intersecting his flight path to the pit.

A week later, on Friday afternoon when we left school in Bel Air, we stopped by for a visit at the local sporting goods store, which back in those days meant Ike Archer's place at the corner of Harford and Belair Roads. Ike was a real sportsman and his place was the kind of a store that the collectors of today would love to be able to step back into. It was a warm, cozy sort of a store and a lot of that atmosphere was attributable to Ike himself. Though he seldom moved from behind his desk, he was always friendly and open with advice to young hunters and fishermen. His whole store always reminded me of a large den in someone's home. Ike at his desk and the far wall covered with a rack full of old shotguns, doubles of all makes and descriptions, used and reconditioned, just waiting to be examined by eager young hands with the dream of a possible purchase one day foremost in our minds. The other walls were covered with memorabilla and artifacts, mounted water fowl, quail, and squirrels, wildlife paintings, turtle shells, snake skins, and hornet nests, old gunpowder advertisements, and fishing tackle and plugs of all kinds and ages. An especial attraction that lured me in later years to visit this intriguing hoard of merchandise were the old antique wooden decoys that Ike always had seemingly hidden away on the floor under the gun racks. Soon after my initial introduction to the allure of collecting wooden decoys, I headed for Ike Archer's store and some of the earliest additions to my new found hobby were purchased there for anywhere from fifty cents to two dollars each. A high price, I thought, for an old wooden decoy.

Anyway, on this particular Friday afternoon we had gone to Ike's to look at new things, namely a set of Victor crow and owl decoys made of paper mache that sold for about $5.00 for the two crows and one owl. After relating our last weeks experience to Ike, he allowed as how the decoys would probably do the job of bringing in the crows. During that week we had reread our stack of *Field and Stream, Sports Afield, Outdoor Life,* and *Fur Fish Game* magazines, searching out the articles on crow shooting and poring over each word, and they supported what Ike had said. We pooled our money and bought the decoys and an extra box of 16 guage shells.

The next day being Saturday and our day off, we could hardly contain our excitement at the prospect of another crack at the crows over on Tollgate Road. Last week had been their time to laugh, this week it was our turn. We were up before dawn, as always, and as soon as the chores were done and the cows milked, Charlie and I grabbed the old '38 Chevy pick-up and headed for our rendevous with the crows. We arrived as dawn was breaking and everything was still relatively quiet. We picked a spot on the edge of the wood lot a short distance from the dump, but on what we figured might be the flight path of the crows. We set up our rig, the owl decoy on top of a dead, fairly tall stump - an unlikely site for an owl to perch, but one that we decided would be very conspicuous - and our two lonely crow decoys in branches overlooking the owl. An Olt's crow call completed our equipment and we burrowed down into the honeysuckle to hide. We did not wait long this morning. As the sun rose behind us, the light filtering through the honeysuckle leaves dappled my brother's face as I watched him intently studying the direction from which we hoped the crows would come. Suddenly, he instinctively crouched lower and I saw the black marauder slashing from its path to take a dive at our owl. We gave a couple of calls that sounded not much like a crow, but our visitor immediately took up the hue and cry. He had been heading for breakfast, but fast changed his mind and his tune when he spotted that owl decoy. Before we even knew what was happening the air was full of screaming crows, twisting and darting, and providing us with some exciting wing shooting. The rest of that tale is another story, but the decoys worked, and suffice it to say we had crow pie for supper the following week.

Quite possibly the earliest crow decoy wasn't made until after 1900. If any were made earlier they probably originated on Long Island. Fine crow decoys by William Bowman and Daniel Demott, both from Long Island, are known and these could predate 1900.

The Mason Decoy Company of Detroit, Michigan appears to have produced the earliest of the commercially made crow decoys. None have been identified to date by any of the earlier factories. In the Mason catalog dated 1905, a reproduction of which was published in 1980 by Hal Sorenson, there is no crow decoy listed or shown. In a catalog dated 1912, published by Schoverling, Daly, & Gales in New York, and listing their sportsmen supplies, there is advertised on page 142 a Mason crow decoy selling for $5.00 per dozen. The advertisement states that it is "The finest crow decoy on the market. Cut from a solid wood block, well shaped and painted." "It is becoming popular to shoot crows over decoys, especially in closed season on other birds," the ad goes on to say. This is the earliest reference that I was able to uncover for a factory made crow decoy. The Mason crow seems to be a rare bird indeed and only a few are known in collections today.

William E. Pratt apparently continued to produce wooden crow decoys after he purchased the Mason Decoy Company equipment in 1924. These decoys also turn up all too infrequently. The Herters Company in Waseca, Minnesota turned out very nice balsa wood crow and owl decoys from the 1930's through the 1940's and even these wooden decoys are seldom found today and would be desirable additions to any collection.

After World War II, with the development of new technology, a number of commercial decoy manufacturers began making their birds out of plastic and paper mache. A large number of crow and owl decoys were made of paper mache by Carry-Lite Decoy Company, Animal Trap Company or Victor, and General Fiber Company or Ari-Duck. They were very effective as witnessed by earlier writing in this chapter, and today are just starting to be collected by those interested in the history of hunting and its memorabilia.

The crow shoot was once a very popular sport and it filled the need for the hunter to go afield during the closed season to search for a worthy target. For those who shot a few and tried them on the table, he provided an outdoor engagement as pleasurable as hunting bona fide game birds. For those who sought only the crow's extirpation, it is good that he is now somewhat protected. The fact that the American crow has adapted to and withstood every horror and execrable attempt to eliminate him by the hands of man and yet today remains a prominent figure in our birdlife only manages to prove the words of that eminent scribe, Henry Ward Beecher, when he said "If men wore feathers and wings, very few of them would be clever enough to be crows."

# American Factory Decoys -
# An Alphabetical Guide

## A-B-C BAIT, MFG. CO
Detroit, Michigan

*Ad (Courtesy Hunting & Fishing Magazine.
October 1941.)*

## ACME FOLDING DECOY
St. Louis Brass Manufacturing Company
St. Louis, Missouri

The Acme Folding Decoy was patented
in 1895 by the St. Louis Brass Manufacturing Company in St. Louis, Missouri. They
were offered only in the mallard species
and were made of the "best quality of
canvas, with wood float of white pine."
The canvas was printed in indelible colors
and fastened to the bottom board over a
collapsible wire frame. When the lever on
the side was operated the frame would
erect, filling out the canvas to a full size
duck. They came packed one dozen in a
wooden box which was attractively printed
and had a handle for easy carrying. They
sold for $4.00 a dozen as advertised in the
1902 Sears Roebuck catalog. The price
increased to $7.50 in 1903 and to $9.50 by
1907. A piece of wood is inserted in the
canvas for the bill.

*Acme canvas mallard in the fully formed ready for use position. Note the elaborate painted feather patterns on the canvas. Decoy c-1900. (Collection of the author.*

*Acme Folding canvas drake mallard decoy in the collapsed carrying position. Note the small wire lever along the bottom edge which erects the framework to form the duck. (Collection of the author.)*

# AIRFLATE DECOY CO.

Kansas City, Missouri

*(Courtesy Field & Stream Magazine. November 1940.)*

*(Courtesy Field & Stream Magazine. October 1941.)*

*Ad (Courtesy of Outdoor Life Magazine. October 1925.)*

# AIRTITE DECOY COMPANY
Danville, Illinois

The Airtite Decoy Company began production of their canvas covered rubber decoys in 1923 or 1924 and continued in business for just a short period of time. The reason for their demise seems obvious to the waterfowl hunter. Even other manufacturers of decoys during that period in their ads claimed that a piece of shot or two rendered the inflatable rubber decoys useless. The decoys were made in two pieces, the indelibly printed outer canvas covering and the rubber liner. Along the bottom of the canvas were a series of eyelets that were laced with a cord after the rubber liner had been inserted. A stem was located near the tail and attached to a string was a small stopper that could be fitted into the stem after the decoy was inflated. The birds sold new in 1925 for $30.00 a dozen for ducks, mallard, canvasbacks, and pintail and $48.00 a dozen for "Canadian black goose." By 1927 the prices had dropped to $24.00 a dozen for the ducks and $36.00 a dozen for the geese, perhaps reflecting their unpopularity.

# NEW PRICE ON DECOYS

*Ad (Courtesy of Hunting & Fishing Magazine. October 1927).*

JUMPING DUCKS WITH Allen's Bow-Facer.

**F. A. ALLEN'S IMPROVED DUCK CALLER.**

The most important article in a Duck Shooter's outfit is his Caller. Place two Duck Shooters one-quarter of a mile apart (all other things being equal) and the man with a good Caller will get three times as many good shots as the other shooter will with a poor Caller and ten times as many as a man with no Caller. **F. A. Allen's Duck Call** is the most natural toned, easiest blowing, smallest and only Metal Duck Call ever invented, and is the only Call on the market that perfectly imitates the Wild Duck, as it has none of the nasal twang of the Tame Duck. Amateur Duck Shooters are often deceived, thinking that the Tame Duck Call will successfully call Wild Ducks; when, in fact, the Tame and Wild Duck Calls are no more alike than the Tame and Wild Goose Calls. It is used in the field by all the best duck shooters in America. The 1888 Caller has a new attachment and requires no working of the hand. Sent by mail to any address on receipt of One Dollar. Address,

**FRED. A. ALLEN, Monmouth, Warren Co., Ill.**

### PRICES OF ALLEN'S SPECIALTIES:

Allen's Nickel Plated Duck Call, each $1.00. Allen's Bow-Facing Rowing Gear, per set $6.00. For sale by every Gun Dealer in the U. S. Send for catalogue free.

**WARNING.**—As irresponsible parties in New Jersey have placed on the market a horrible-toned imitation of my Duck Caller, stamped ALLYN, this is to notify all sportsmen and gun dealers that none are of my make unless stamped "F. A. Allen, Monmouth, Ill."

*An advertisement depicting Fred Allen's bow facing oar and his nickel plated duck callers - from* Wild Fowl Shooting *by William D. Leffingwell - 1888.*

## FRED A. ALLEN
Monmouth, Illinois

Although little is known of Fred Allen's decoy making contributions, there are fine small hollow decoys in collections today that are attributed to him. The birds known were hand made, but Fred Allen did enter the commercial field of waterfowling about 1880 with his duck callers, his bow facing oars, and a floating frame that supported dead ducks for use as decoys. These were advertised in several sporting periodicals of the period and at least one book published on wildfowling in 1888. A photo of one of his frames for supporting dead ducks may be seen in Plate 118 on page 159 of *The Decoys and Decoy Carvers of Illinois* by Paul Parmalee and Forrest Loomis.

## ANDERSON DECOYS
San Francisco, California

Several examples of hollow bodied sheet metal pintails with "ANDERSON" in raised letters in the bottom have been discovered and information previously published indicates that they were manufactured by the B. C. Metal Stamping Company located in San Francisco, California. The decoys were produced for a short period of time in the late 1920's and only pintails are known.

*This photograph accompanied a story of duck hunting in the San Joaquin Valley in California in 1923. The decoy on the extreme right in the photo appears to be an Anderson metal decoy.*

*Anderson pintail decoy made of hollow tin with the impressed name "ANDERSON DECOY" in the bottom. (Collection of Ted Harmon.)*

*Bottom of the Anderson pintail.*

*Another hollow tin or sheet metal pintail decoy just about identical in style to the Anderson decoy, but with the name "BAKER DECOY" in raised letters on the bottom. (Collection of Ted Harmon.)*

*Bottom of the Baker decoy.*

26

## ANIMAL TRAP COMPANY OF AMERICA
### Lititz, Pennsylvania

When William E. Pratt died in 1939, his manufacturing company which specialized in iron castings and hardware was sold to the Joslyn Manufacturing Company. They in turn sold the decoy, mouse, and rat trap departments to the Animal Trap Company of America in Lititz, Pennsylvania, a long established firm that produced animal traps for catching furbearers. The decoy brand name was changed to Victor and the plant in Lititz continued making wooden decoys until sometime in 1942, when the full efforts of the company were directed toward the war effort. Subsequent to the purchase of the decoy department from the William E. Pratt Company, the Animal Trap Company purchased the Poitevin Brothers decoy operation in Pascagoula, Mississippi and formed a subsidiary to the parent company there for the purpose of manufacturing wooden lathe turned birds. At least five different decoy producing companies have been recorded as having been located in Pascagoula, a location chosen for its natural abundance of tupelo gum and pop ash. These two woods, native to the Singing River country of lower

Mississippi, are extremely buoyant, light weight, and plentiful; they proved very suitable for the manufacture of decoys. The Poitevin Brothers decoys, before the purchase of Animal Trap Company, were sold under the brand name of "Singing River Decoys." After the war, in 1946, a ruinous fire completely destroyed the Animal Trap Company's plant and all of its equipment, temporarily shutting down the Mississippi decoy operations. At that same time or a year earlier, Animal Trap purchased the Hudson Decoy Company, also located in Pascagoula, adding the Vac-Sta and Duo-Sta brand to the Victor line, and with this company resumed wooden decoy production in Mississippi which continued until 1962. As far as can be determined by the research on the part

*"Pascagoula Decoys" - Left is a pair of pintails by Animal Trap Company of Mississippi and to the right is a pair by the Pascagoula Decoy Company, two separate companies operating in Pascagoula. In the left foreground is an Animal Trap Company of Mississippi bluebill with the Vac-Sta bottom and straight line rubber stamp. On the right is a solid Animal Trap bluebill with the round rubber stamp. (Collection of the author.)*

*Animal Trap Company black duck in original paint.*
*(Collection of the author.)*

of the author, two different decoy making companies survived in Pascagoula and continued turning out their product there until the early 1960's. They were the Animal Trap Company of Mississippi, who bought first Poitevin Brothers and then the Hudson Company, turning out wooden birds under the Victor brand, and the Pascagoula Decoy Company making their birds under the "Padco" brand. It appears that these two enterprises were never associated in any way, as both were advertising as separate companies in national sporting magazines until the late 1950's and early 1960's. Advertisements for decoys did not appear after 1942 and all during the war, but began appearing again in 1945 when the wooden "Vac-Sta" decoys were offered in ten different species: mallard, red hen (probably a mistake and meant to be red head,) canvasback, pintail, bluebill, black duck, teal, widgeon, whistler, and mud hen. Both this ad in *Outdoor Life,* October 1945 and the *Field and Stream* ad of December 1951 offer the free folder, which is illustrated in this article entitled "How to Use Duck Decoys Successfully." The owner of this little brochure received it in the 1950's. The wood used for manufacture of the Victor decoys was the southern pop ash and tupelo gum mentioned earlier as being abundant in the Singing River country of lower Mississippi. They were also offered in balsa wood. Again, one must guess at the dates that decoys made of new materials were offered, but it appears that the end of World War II brought the cellulose-plastic decoy into the Victor line under the trademark of "Veri-lite." Whether cellulose-plastic is another term for what we all know as paper mache is unclear at this point, but the author's conjecture is that it is. First, the photos in the ads of the cellulose-plastic Veri-lites are identical to the early paper mache mallards and black ducks that Victor offered; second, the trade mark "VERI-LITE" is impressed in the bottom of these paper mache decoys along with the the date 1946; third, no one has seen any other kind of a Victor decoy that could be classed as cellulose-plastic. The paper mache decoys have always had little value or interest to decoy collectors, but a blue wing teal listed as composition and impressed "VICTOR VERI-LITE,

1946" on the bottom, sold for $25.00 in session VI of the Mackey auction in 1974. It is safe to say that there would be enough collectors interested in such a bird today that should it be offered for sale it would easily double its 1974 price.

Around 1952 Victor Animal Trap Company offered molded tenite decoys, a hard plastic material that was used to produce hollow decoys that often filled with water and sank when hit by an errant piece of shot. During this same period of time wooden bodied decoys with removable tenite heads were presented to the decoy buying public. Not many of these birds are found today which leads to the supposition that they were not as popular as the other offerings and were produced for only a short period of time. A pair of canvasbacks, several pintails, and a mallard drake are illustrated in this section.

The wooden Victor decoys were made in several different models. One of the most easily distinguished characteristics for identification were the blade marks encircling the body that were left showing to give the effect of feathering. All of the models definitely documented as Animal Trap decoys were simply painted, by hand initially and later by airbrush. They were made in a full size standard model, and an oversize model, both hollow and solid. An economy model was very thin and as Charlie Frank stated in his article, was thought by many of us to be a wing duck. The hollow models were bored through the breast for lightening and then sealed with a wooden plug. The Vac-Sta had twin air spaces gouged out alongside each other in the bottom. This produced a lighter and more stable decoy. Many of the wooden Animal Trap decoys have the brand name of 'VICTOR" branded in the bottom. In later years a rubber stamp with the name "ANIMAL TRAP CO. of MISSISSIPPI, INC. PASCAGOULA, MISS." was imprinted in ink on the bottom.

The heads on these decoys were also turned on a duplicating lathe and the circular blade marks on them were very evident. All of the heads were drilled and fitted with glass eyes and were attached to the bodies with a one half inch grooved wooden dowel. Many of the heads were left loose and free to turn in any position, while others were glued straight ahead or turned slightly to the right or left.

During the 1960's the Animal Trap Company of America changed its name, which was instituted in 1896, to the Woodstream Corporation, thus a name that we all grew up with was reduced to mere history. In 1966, all of the molded fibre decoys except for the Canada goose were discontinued and in 1971 the Mississippi plant at Pascagoula was closed forever. Agnes, the devastating hurricane of 1972 flooded the offices of the Animal Trap Company at Lititz, Pennsylvania and destroyed finally all of the old decoy records and catalogs. At least the name of Victor, which originated as the name of a steel trap in 1886, lives on. For someone looking for an inexpensive and rather interesting direction in which to begin his decoy collecting, the long line of decoys of the Animal Trap Company of America just might be the answer for him.

My thanks go to Dave Morrison, President of Woodstream Corporation, and Charlie Frank for portions of this information.

A nice pair of Victor Animal Trap 1946 paper mache goldeneyes. These birds were made at the Lititz, Pennsylvania plant initially, starting right after the war, and listed as Victor Veri-Lites made of cellulose plastic. (Collection of the author.)

These oversize canvasback decoys were made by the Animal Trap Company of Mississippi at Pascagoula sometime during their wood production years, but no one seems to know for sure just when. (Collection of the author.)

Five Victor Veri-Lite decoys made about 1946 in Lititz, Pennsylvania. In new original condition they were purchased after the war by the old Samis and Bray Sporting Goods Store in Easton, Maryland and sold at a yard sale of sporting goods that was held in 1974 when the late Mr. Samis sold his storage building. (Collection of the author.)

A Victor Animal Trap Company decoy showing the Victor brand in the bottom along with the old Samis and Bray Sporting Goods Store stencil. (Collection of the author.)

*A Victor black duck, long and slender, and probably a "cull" grade decoy, which was Victor's lowest priced decoy. (Collection of the author.)*

*A mint original condition Animal Trap Company wooden mallard decoy with a removable tenite head. Offered about 1952 when Victor began making tenite decoys. (Collection of the author.)*

*The economy model No. 12 offered by the Animal Trap Company. A thinner piece of wood was used for this model which helped to reduce the cost of the decoy. (Collection of the author.)*

*A pair of the economical Victor bluebills with wooden keels and ballast weight added by the hunter who owned and used them. (Collection of the author.)*

*A Victor No. 12 hen mallard in mint original condition. The very simplest paint patterns employed on these birds helped maintain the low cost, about $4.50 a dozen. (Collection of the author.)*

*Part of a rig of mint original condition diving duck decoys by Victor Animal Trap of Mississippi. Found in Talbot County, Maryland by the author, they included canvasbacks, redheads, blackheads, whistler, and widgeon. (Collection of the author.)*

*An original condition bluebill decoy by the Animal Trap Company of Mississippi made at the factory with a turned sleeping or preening head. (Collection of Ted Harmon.)*

*A pair of Victor Veri-Lite blue wing teal in completely original condition. (Collection of Dan Brown.)*

*The bottoms of the preceding Victor teal showing the Victor Veri-Lite name and date of 1946.*

*A pair of Victor Animal Trap canvasbacks made c-1952 with wooden bodies and tenite heads. (Collection of the Author.)*

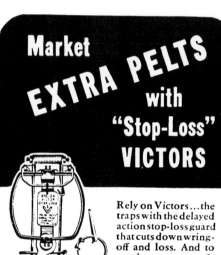

*Ad displaying the Victor Animal Trap Company's
crow shooter kit and some of their duck hunting
accessories.*

*Ad (Courtesy of National Sportsman Magazine.
November 1941.)*

*Ad (Courtesy of Sports Afield Magazine.
October 1946.)*

*Ad (Courtesy of Outdoor Life Magazine.
October 1945.)*

# HOW TO USE
## DUCK DECOYS
### *Successfully*

**ANIMAL TRAP COMPANY OF MISSISSIPPI**

*Subsidiary of*

**ANIMAL TRAP COMPANY OF AMERICA**

Lititz, Penna.    Pascagoula, Miss.    Niagara Falls, Ont.

## DECOY ACCESSORIES

### No. I VICTOR DECOY ANCHOR

Designed to unreel the amount of line required—additional line let out automatically in a rising tide. When decoys are lifted simply wrap the line around prongs and slip anchor over head of decoy, eliminating tangled lines in car and boat. Weight 14 ounces each.

### No. I VICTOR DECOY Balance Weight

The ultimate in simplicity and design. One screw fastens weight to body. Adjust to position and tighten—two small prongs prevent balance from changing position. Weight 8 ounces each. (Do not use on Victor Veri-Lite decoys.)

### No. 4 VICTOR MUSHROOM ANCHOR

Years of service have proven the popularity and dependability of this anchor. Tie anchor line to hole in upright stem. Weight 8 ounces each.

### No. 4 VICTOR BODY WEIGHT

This body weight has an eyelet for anchor line. Weight is easily attached to decoy with either two nails or screws. Weight 4 ounces each. (Do not use on Victor Veri-Lite Decoys.)

*Distributed by*

**UNIVERSAL TACKLE & SPTG. GOODS CORP.
151 WEST 19TH STREET
NEW YORK, NEW YORK**

PRINTED IN U.S.A.                    R—5-50—5M

---

# VICTOR
## VERI-LITE DECOYS

Here is the genuine duck shooter's Decoy. The *Victor Veri-Lite Decoy* is a cellulose-plastic that is light enough to tote over the marsh without fatigue. *Victor Veri-Lite Decoys* are lifelike reproductions of wildfowl; copied from real ducks by a sculptor of national reputation. These decoys are full size, thoroughly waterproof and made to stand hard usage.

*Victor Veri-Lite Decoys* are balanced at the factory and equipped with anchor line swivel. No tedious preparations—just tie on your line and they're ready to use.

**All Victor Decoys are furnished in Mallard, Black Duck, Pintail, Red Head, Canvasback, Blue Bill, Widgeon, Whistler and Teal.**

**Order your requirements from your Dealer now.**

### DUCK HUNTERS—HELP YOUR SPORT

No organization of sportsmen is doing more for the restoration of our waterfowl and the sport of wildfowling than Ducks Unlimited, Inc. Every real duck hunter can help this national wildfowler's organization by becoming a member. Write Ducks Unlimited, Inc., 342 Madison Avenue, New York 17, N. Y. for membership literature.

## WOOD DECOYS

### VICTOR WOOD DECOYS

Produced from buoyant Southern pop ash down in the Singing River Country of lower Mississippi where decoy making is a tradition. This is the old reliable solid wood decoy that has been used for years wherever ducks are shot.

### VICTOR VAC STA DECOYS

The choice of duck shooters that want a wood decoy to ride high on the water. *Twin Vacuum Cups* reduce weight and keep decoy upright without use of weights.

### VICTOR BALSA DECOYS

The deluxe decoy for discriminating duck shooters. Manufactured from Balsa—the most buoyant and lightest wood known. Painted in dull colors to eliminate glare. *Victor Balsa Decoys* are sold at popular prices. Balsa goose decoys custom made to order.

## NET DEALERS PRICES
### —ON—
# DECOY ACCESSORIES
### June 1, 1939
(Subject to change without notice)

---

### DECOY HEADS

Heads made from fine grained pine. This type of wood was selected after careful investigation and experiment. Heads with eyes, complete with dowel for replacing damaged heads, are available in all sizes and type. Packed — according to orders. Sizes either Nos. 1, 2 or 12. Be sure to specify type of duck and finish for which heads are being ordered. Also specify whether heads are for drake or hen.
Price per dozen .......................................... $3.20

EYES

### DECOY EYES

Supplied for all types. Specify type of decoy for which eyes are desired.
Price per dozen pairs ................................... $ .40

### DECOY ANCHORS

**No. 1A** — Cast Iron — So designed that after cord has been wound around neck, large anchor loop can be slipped over head of decoy for storing. Weight each 7 ounces.
Price per dozen ........................................ $ .90

**No. 1B** — Galvanized — Same style as No. 1A except for finish.
Price per dozen ........................................ $1.15

No. 1A and No. 1B

**No. 4A** — Mushroom type — Cast Iron with hole in upright stem for tying cord. Weight each 8 ounces.
Price per dozen ........................................ $1.15

**No. 4B** — Same mushroom type as No. 4A except for size. Weight each 18 ounces.
Price per dozen ........................................ $2.35

No. 4A and No. 4B

### BALANCE WEIGHTS FOR DECOYS

Cast Iron with eyelets for anchor cord. Two nail holes for fastening weight to decoy. These weights are easily attached and will balance the decoy so it will set upright properly in water. Cheaper than lead strips and no trouble to attach.

**No. 4** — Japanned finish — For all standard solid decoys. Packed 1 dozen to a box, weight each 4 ounces.
Price per dozen ........................................ $ .95

**No. 5** — Japanned finish — For all hollow and larger decoys. Packed 1 dozen to a box, weight each 12 ounces.
Price per dozen ........................................ $1.60

No. 4 and No. 5

**No. 6** — Cast Iron — Fitted with lugs so weight may be fastened to decoys. Made like keel of a boat. Will keep decoy upright in rough water. Packed 1 dozen to a box, weight each 4 ounces.
Price per dozen ........................................ $ .80

No. 6

### DECOY ANCHOR CORD

Supplied with all orders for decoy anchors and weights. Twelve only, 8 foot cords in each package.

---

Dealers and sportsmen should be notified by wholesalers' salesmen that we maintain a service for repairing, repainting and replacing of broken heads, damaged or missing eyes. Write for quotations, giving details of necessary repairs. Quotations will be mailed same day request is received. All work properly handled.

# ANIMAL TRAP COMPANY OF AMERICA
## LITITZ, PA.

See other side for Price List and Description of Decoys

*(Courtesy of Dave Morrison.)*

# NET DEALERS PRICES

## —ON—

# VICTOR DECOYS

### June 1, 1939

(Subject to change without notice)

Made from selected water resisting lumber — Heads and bodies carefully painted true to nature
Highest grade of machine made decoys — Fine grade glass eyes

Victor Decoys are manufactured in the following species, in each of the 3 types — Nos. 1, 2 and 12.

| | | | |
|---|---|---|---|
| **MALLARD** | **REDHEAD** | **PINTAIL** (Sprig) | **WIDGEON** |
| **CANVASBACK** | **TEAL** | **BLUE BILL** (Broadbill) | **WHISTLER** |
| | **BLACK DUCK** (Black Mallard) | **MUD HEN** (Amer. Coot) | |

In description below we have used Mallard type as example to show length — Height is in proportion on each decoy. Dimensions and weights will vary slightly according to species.

## DUCK DECOYS

(Packed ½ dozen to case — 4 Drakes — 2 Hens)

| | | Length Inches | Approximate Shipping Wt. per ½ doz. Solid | Hollow | Price Per Dozen — F.O.B. Lititz, Pa. Sanded Finish Solid | Sanded Finish Hollow | Feather Finish Solid | Feather Finish Hollow |
|---|---|---|---|---|---|---|---|---|
| No. 1 | Standard Size. This is the De-Luxe Finish in the Decoy Line .. | 14 | 16 lbs. | 13 lbs. | $ 8.35 | $ 9.00 | $ 7.65 | $ 8.35 |
| No. 2 | Mammoth Size. Produced in our Premier Finish, both as to paint and construction ........... | 15 | 20 lbs. | 17 lbs. | $13.35 | $14.00 | $12.65 | $14.00 |
| No. 12 | Feather Finish only. This is the Decoy for meeting all price competition. Well made, carefully painted, true to natural coloring of type .................. | 13 | 12 lbs. | 10 lbs. | — | — | $ 6.00 | $ 6.65 |

## GOOSE DECOYS

(Packed ½ dozen to reshipping carton — 4 Ganders — 2 Hens)

| | | Length Inches | Approximate Shipping Wt. Per ½ Doz. | Sanded Solid | Sanded Hollow |
|---|---|---|---|---|---|
| No. 5 | Extra large, sanded finish. Goose Decoy only. Produced in our Premier Finish, both as to paint and construction .............. | 17 | 25 lbs. | $26.65 | $32.00 |

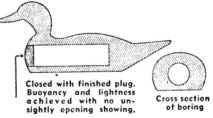

Closed with finished plug. Buoyancy and lightness achieved with no unsightly opening showing.

Cross section of boring

This type Hollow Decoy has been produced by W. E. Pratt Manufacturing Company for over 15 years and has met wide-spread acceptance.

# ANIMAL TRAP COMPANY OF AMERICA

## LITITZ, PA.

**See other side for Prices and Descriptions of Accessories**

*(Courtesy of Dave Morrison.)*

## ARMSTRONG CORK COMPANY
Pittsburgh, Pennsylvania

The Armstrong Cork Company made decoys during the late 1920's and early 1930's, but the exact dates of the beginning of decoy production and its end are unknown. The bodies were made of cork insulating board from Beaver Falls, Pennsylvania and they were spray painted with an airbrush. The heads were made by a separate concern in New England and were painted there before being shipped to Pittsburgh for assembly. They were doweled to the cork bodies. The birds were made from June to September during the cork company's off season. They made only mallard decoys. This information and the decoy in the photograph are presented here through the courtesy of Sam Dyke of Salisbury, Maryland.

## ARMSTRONG FEATHERWEIGHT DECOYS
Houston, Texas

The Armstrong Featherweight Decoys were made of a canvas covering printed mechanically with an elaborate rendition of the species coloration and feathering and filled with kapok or ground cork. The bodies were sewn through the back with a heavy waxed cord presumably to help hold them together so that they might withstand hard usage. A tapered wooden bill was inserted in its proper place in the canvas for the beak. Glass eyes are found in all of the birds. Apparently two different models were made and the later birds did not have the waxed cord sewn through their bodies. Otherwise, they were very similar in construction and style. The exact dates for the beginning and end of the company are not known, but they advertised extensively during the years 1939-1941. Advertised for sale were mallards, pintails, bluebills, black mallards, Canada goose, and white goose.

*A hen mallard decoy made by the Armstrong Cork Company, Pittsburgh, Pennsylvania-c.-1930. (Collection of Sam Dyke.)*

*(Courtesy Hunting & Fishing Magazine - October 1940).*

*(Courtesy Sports Afield Magazine - November 1940).*

**MALLARDS—PINTAILS**

**MALLARD DRAKE**
PAT. PENDING

**Generations have waited for a Decoy like this**
Lightweight—Average 8 oz. Flat bottom, no body weight or counterbalance needed except in very rough water. Practically indestructible, given reasonable care will last indefinitely. Completely waterproof. Lifelike swimming action. Mechanically printed. Visible at great distances. Anchor rings attached. Two piece construction. Hand stitched to shape. Fully guaranteed.

Samples $1.50 each. Dozen $16.50 Delivered in U. S. A. Order direct if your dealer can't supply you.

Jobbers and dealers write us.

**ARMSTRONG FEATHERWEIGHT DECOYS**
**400 Citizens State Bank Building, Houston, Texas**

*(Courtesy Field & Stream Magazine - October 1939).*

**Wild Fowl Are Smart**

MALLARD DRAKE

But no duck or goose is smart enough to tell Armstrong FEATHERWEIGHTS from the real thing—until it's too late.

Armstrong FEATHERWEIGHT Decoys are such true-life reproductions of the wild birds that your hunting success will be assured. Armstrong FEATHERWEIGHTS are easy to carry before and after the hunt. Weight of decoys averages less than 1/2 lb. each, yet ride the water like real birds. Full life-size, in natural colors that won't shine. Long-lasting. Will not sink if shot. No yearly repainting necessary. Scientifically made by hand, and carefully balanced.

Featherweights, Feeders, and the new 12-bird combination of Featherweights and Feeders. Choice of 4 species, Mallards, Pintails, Bluebills, and Black Mallards. Featherweights $13.50 Doz. Sample $1.25 each. 12-Bird Combination $10.00. Sample (4) $4.00. New Improved Duck-In Feeders $6.00. Sample (2) $1.25. Canada Goose $3.00 each. White Goose $2.50 each. 10% higher west of Rocky Mountains. *Order direct if your dealer can't supply you.*

**ARMSTRONG FEATHERWEIGHT DECOYS, INC.**
**400-A Citizens State Bank Building,** Houston, Texas

*(Courtesy Field & Stream Magazine - November 1941).*

Advertisement for Armstrong Featherweight Decoys.

# FOR **BETTER** HUNTING!
## ARMSTRONG *Featherweight* DECOYS

MALLARD DRAKE

**TRULY LIFELIKE— THEY SWIM!**

WEIGHT OF DECOYS AVERAGES LESS THAN 1/2 LB. EACH!

## LIGHT IN WEIGHT—LOW IN COST!

The better the decoy—the better the hunting! That's why duck hunters everywhere prefer true-to-life Armstrong FEATHERWEIGHTS. Extremely light, yet they ride the water like real birds. Easy to carry before and after the hunt. Full life-size, in natural colors that won't shine. Long-lasting. Will not sink if shot. No yearly repainting necessary. Scientifically made by hand and carefully balanced. Featherweights, Feeders, and the 12-bird combination of Featherweights and Feeders. Choice of 4 species: Mallards, Pintails, Bluebills, and Black Mallards.

**PRICES:** Featherweights $15.00 Doz. Sample $1.50 each. 12-bird Combination $10.50. Sample (4) $4.25. New Improved Duck-in Feeders $7.50 Doz. Sample (2) $1.50. Canada Goose $3.35 each. White Goose $3.00 each. Other direct if your dealer can't supply you.

**ORDER YOUR FEATHERWEIGHTS TODAY**

**ARMSTRONG FEATHERWEIGHT DECOYS, INC.**
**Citizens State Bank Bldg., Houston, Texas**
**ORDER SHIPPED ON DAY RECEIVED**

*(Courtesy Sports Afield Magazine - October 1941).*

**STOP** *the highflyers with*
ARMSTRONG *Featherweight* DECOYS

SPRIG DRAKE

**TRULY LIFELIKE— THEY SWIM!**

**Weight of Decoys averages about 1/2 lb. each!**
Armstrong *FEATHERWEIGHT* Decoys are visible at great distances; are extremely light in weight, yet ride the water like real birds. Fast colors that will not shine. Carefully waterproofed—cannot fill with water and therefore will not freeze solid and become heavy. Preferred by duck hunters everywhere. Choice of 4 species: Mallards, Pintails, Bluebills, and Black Mallards.

*PRICES:* Featherweights $15.00 doz. Sample $1.50 each. New Improved Duck-in Feeders $7.50 doz. Sample (2) $1.50. 12-bird Combination $10.50. Sample (4) $4.25. Canada Goose $3.35 each. White Goose $3.00 each. Order direct if your dealer cannot supply you. (Order shipped on day received.)

**Armstrong Featherweight Decoys, Inc.**
**Citizens State Bank Bldg., Houston, Texas**

*(Courtesy Sports Afield Hunting Annual 1940).*

**M100 Mallard Drake**

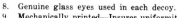

**M101 Mallard Hen**

**ARMSTRONG FEATHERWEIGHT LIFE LIKE DECOYS**

Just think! 50 full sized decoys only weigh 28 lbs. Here are the reasons:

1. They are truly life-like.
2. Action on the Water—"They Swim."
3. Visibility—Visibility equal to that of wild bird.
4. Flat bottom — ride on top of water, without body weight.
5. Completely waterproofed—Will not gain weight from absorption.
6. Anchor ring attached to each decoy.
7. Practically non-destructive—Head, Bills, or Tails will not break off in handling or rough use.
8. Genuine glass eyes used in each decoy.
9. Mechanically printed—Insures uniformity and accurate color design.
10. They are hand made and carefully balanced.
11. Fully Guaranteed.

M100 Mallard Drake    S106 Pintail Hen
M101 Mallard Hen    B109 Black Duck
S105 Pintail Drake

**Each, $1 60**

**D-45—New Duck-In Decoy.** Headless type. In use they look like feeding decoys. Supplied in Mallard Drake or Mallard Hen. 5 or 6 pounds weight to a dozen. Each          $0 85

An Armstrong featherweight pintail hen in almost mint condition. (Collection of Dan Brown.)

An Armstrong featherweight canvas covered Canada goose decoy in original condition. (Collection of Morton and Carol Kramer.)

**ARTIN'S DECOYS**
Milwaukee, Wisconsin

Bluebill decoy by Artin's Decoys, Milwaukee, Wisconsin. (Collection of Morton and Carol Kramer.)

Bottom of preceding decoy showing stencil of name and location.

*Captain Chip Allsopp working on the lathe which turns the heads and bodies for Barnegat Bay Decoys.*

*Art Birdsall, a direct decendent of the famous decoy making Birdsalls of New Jersey, working in the sanding area at Barnegat Bay Decoys.*

## BALSA KING DECOY
Belmont, California

## BARNEGAT BAY DECOYS
Point Pleasant, New Jersey

When Charles Birdsall sold his Wildfowler decoy operation at Point Pleasant, New Jersey, all of the equipment and the Wildfowler name moved to Babylon, New York into the ownership of Amel and Karen Massa. Rick Brown bought Charlie's home and shop, retooled the shop, and began the Barnegat Bay Decoy Company, much in the same tradition as the Wildfowler Company. Rick, with the help of Art Birdsall, Chip Allsopp, and Tim Forsyth produce quality hunting decoys made of white cedar and decorative birds for use on lamps and as items for Ducks Unlimited auctions.

*The crew at Barnegat Bay Decoys, from the left-Art Birdsall, owner Rick Brown, Tim Forsyth, and Captain Chip Allsopp.*

## BATES DECOYS
Cambridge, Massachusetts

Bates decoys are canvas covered kapok, excelsior, or a similar material. The bodies were machine sewn except along the bottom seam where they were sewn by hand. Ballast was incorporated into the bottom of the canvas by stitching around a circular lead weight and there is a round imprinted name and location of the company "BATES BREAKPROOF DECOYS, PAT. PENDING , CAMBRIDGE, MASS." The paint patterns were rather nicely done and the heads detached from the body by means of a snap. The decoys shown are in the collection of Ted Harmon of Barnstable, Massachusetts and I thank him for permission to take the photos.

*Bates Breakproof Canvas Decoys - A pair of goldeneyes in the foreground and a bluebill drake in the background.*

44

## BAYCO DECOY COMPANY
New Orleans, Louisiana

A search for information on this decoy company or for a photo of one of the decoys was to no avail. Apparently successful, advertisements were found from 1923 and 1930 indicating at least a seven year run - no one had any knowledge of the Bayco Decoy Company.

## L. L. BEAN, INC.
Freeport, Maine

Since the 1950's my brother and I have looked forward to receiving the various catalogs from L.L. Bean, Inc. in Freeport, Maine. When our Christmas or birthday lists were made out, a new pair of Maine hunting boots or brush pants was sure to be included by one of us. Their products have always been of the best quality, well fitted, and reasonably priced. Any problems with any of their merchandise was handled promptly and with the kindest courtesies. L. L. Bean continued to live up to its tradition of excellent customer relations when I requested information on the decoys that they have been selling for many years through their catalog. L.L. Bean has offered George Soule's fine cork decoys for sale since about 1935, when George first designed the Coastal Model black duck for himself and Mr. Bean to hunt over. George went into business back then to produce the Coastal Model and Oversized Model birds that have come to be known as L. L. Bean decoys even though they have been sold by other companies through the years. The Decoy Shop, owned and operated by George until recent years, always made their decoys from cork with a white pine head and inset pine or masonite tail. Those original birds he made were of cork and George has always contended that there is no finer material for decoy making. The Decoy Shop today is owned by Mr. Hargy Heap who continues in George Soule's footsteps to manufacture estimable over-sized decoys for sale through L. L. Bean, Inc.

## Bean's Goose Decoy

This extra large Cork Goose Decoy will make a very attractive addition to any stool of Black Duck or Mallard decoys. One or two Goose Decoys set out along with the regular decoys tend to make the birds less wary. It was judged winner in the Goose Decoy class at the National Decoy Contest. Length, 22"; width, 9¾"; weight, approx. 4 lbs. Made with either solid or patented removable head. Price each, $8.70 postpaid. Set of 6, $49.50. Write for Fall Catalog.

**L.L.Bean,Inc.,162 Main St.,Freeport, Maine**
*Mfrs. of Hunting and Camping Specialties*

Ad (Courtesy of Field & Stream Magazine. December 1956.)

## Bean's Mallard Cork Decoys

Featuring the new removable head which we believe to be the biggest advancement in decoys in years. Completely does away with head breakage while carrying and less space required for packing. Made with extra large cork body and pine bottom. Will not glisten in sun when wet. Complete with snap, anchor line and built-in body weight. Price $1.80 postpaid. Write for catalog showing 3 other patterns.

**Manufactured by**
**L. L. Bean, Inc., 162 Main Street, Freeport, Maine**
**Mfrs. Hunting & Camping Specialties**

Ad (Courtesy of Field & Stream. October 1941.)

*A black duck rig of Bean's famous Deluxe Oversized decoys. (Photo courtesy of L. L. Bean, Inc.)*

L.L.Bean Coastal Model decoys produced for
years by George Soule of _The Decoy Shop_ and
sold through L.L.Bean catalogs. (Photo courtesy of L.L.Bean, Inc.)

A pair of early George Soule mallard decoys made
for L.L.Bean, Inc. (Collection of Morton and Carol
Kramer.)

*An L.L.Bean cork miniature blackbuck - sold as a decorative item for sportsmens dens and game rooms, these little birds were close replicas of their full sized hunting counterparts. (Collection of the author.)*

*A Coastal Model mallard drake and black duck made by George Soule for L.L. Bean, Inc. These birds were bought in the late 50's and saw a number of years of service on the Choptank River in Dorchester County, Maryland. (Collection of the author.)*

## BENZ DECOYS
Jefferson City, Missouri

This company was apparently either the predecessor or successor to the J. M. Hays Decoy Company. There is no date on the circular reproduced here and trying to discover whether they were before or after Hays proved to no avail. They offered the same "Grand Prix" and "Superior" grade duck decoy models and the cut of their goose decoy in the advertisement is identical to the cut in the Hays catalog.

The only comparison between the respective company's advertising materials that could prove to be a clue is the cost of a dozen pair of glass eyes. The Hays catalog lists them at $.60 per dozen pair, while the Benz circular shows them at $.25 per dozen pair. This demonstrates that possibly the Benz circular and decoys are earlier than the Hays.

# BENZ *Lifelike* DECOYS
## JEFFERSON CITY, MISSOURI

### GRAND PRIX MODEL

Special light-weight wood, selected especially for decoy-making. The Grand Prix Model is larger than life-size. Finished semi-smooth. Heads glued on with ⅝-inch dowels. Dipped two coats primer. Colors hand-painted life-like feather-finish; glass eyes. Size: 17 inches tip to tip; body 5½ inches wide. Weight: 25 lbs. to dozen. Floats and rides the water like a live duck.

### SUPERIOR MODEL

This model is the same size as the Grand Prix, except somewhat flatter and weighs 20 lbs. to the doz. Will ride water nearly as high as the Grand Prix.

★

BOTH
**GRAND PRIX**
AND
**SUPERIOR MODELS**
Made in the Following
Species:
MALLARD
BLACK MALLARD
BLUE BILL (Smaller Body)
PINTAIL
GOLDEN EYE or
WHISTLER
WIDGEON
CANVAS BACK
TEAL (Smaller Body)
RED HEAD

### ACCESSORIES

Heads ready to put on body, drilled for dowel and dowel furnished; drilled for eyes and eyes furnished, but not painted. $2.50 per doz. Eyes, 25c per doz. pair. We are equipped to repair and paint ducks shipped to us, at a reasonable rate. Order early.

### CANADA GOOSE

Special light-weight wood is also used in this decoy. Larger than life-size. Finished semi-smooth and painted true to color. Grand Prix Model only. Weight: 4¼ lbs. each.

*Advertising circular for Benz "Lifelike" decoys-*
*date unknown. (Collection of Joe French.)*

## BOUTIN PRODUCTS
Minneapolis, Minnesota

A product of considerable thought and imagination, this decoy may have been one of those ideas conceived on a slow day in the blind. The bird is constructed of cork with a one inch wooden bottom board and a wooden head with an opening in the top of the head from which the quacking call reaches out to the unsuspecting ducks. a long rubber tube is attached to a piece of metal tubing in the bottom of the decoy and reaches back to the hunter in his blind. A squeeze on a syringe type ball on the end of the rubber tube produces the quacking call out at the decoy. It was first advertised in 1940 and was still being offered by Abercrombie & Fitch in 1948.

*Ad (Courtesy of Sports Afield. 1940)*

*Ad (Courtesy of Sports Afield. October 1941)*

*Original Boutin quacking black duck with a rubber stamp on the bottom identifying it as manufactured by Leo Boutin. (Collection of Morton and Carol Kramer.)*

## BOYD MARTIN DECOY COMPANY
Delphi, Indiana

These decoys were made of printed cloth patterns sewn together so that when they were stuffed with any suitable material they took the form of a crow and owl. When empty, as many as a dozen could easily be carried in a coat pocket.

*Ad (Courtesy of Outdoor Life Magazine. June 1936.)*

*Ad (Courtesy of National Sportsman Magazine. April 1938.)*

## BRINKOP DUCK DECOY

The Brinkop metal duck decoy owes part of its distinction to being advertised in the 1894-95 issue of the Montgomery Ward catalog. It is constructed of hollow sheet metal, the body and head separate pieces, and mounted on a wooden float board. A rather elaborate paint pattern was applied.

*Advertisement in the 1894-95 issue of Montgomery Wards catalog.*

*An original condition hen mallard Brinkop decoy. (Collection of Roger Ludwig.)*

## BUILDERS WOODWORK COMPANY

Burlington, Iowa

Nothing is known of the decoys of this company and as far as has been discovered by the author, no one is even sure what the birds looked like.

*Ad (Courtesy of Field & Stream Magazine. November 1934.)*

## CANVAS DECOY COMPANY
Union City, Tennessee

The advertisement claims the company had been in business for thirty seven years, but as far as is known, no decoys by this company have yet been identified. Certainly there must be a few around if they were making decoys from 1886 until at least 1923.

## CARRY-LITE DECOYS

Milwaukee, Wisconsin

Composition paper decoys or paper mache, as they are commonly referred to, have enjoyed little or no interest among decoy collectors until very recently. With the increasing interest of the history minded collector, birds such as those made by Carry-Lite Decoys are attaining their slot in the annals of decoy production. The Carry-Lite is listed as one of the earliest molded paper birds, having been first manufactured in 1939. Many thousands of these decoys were produced in five species of ducks and Canada goose and shipped to all parts of this country. The earlier birds have the name "Carry-Lite" stenciled on the bottom and the later decoys, after World War II, had the name and address impressed into the decoy bottom during the molding.

*An interesting attachment offered by the Molded Carry-Lite Company in 1940. One would guess this to be a less than practical application and as such probably saw little usage among waterfowl hunters. Ad (Courtesy of Sports Afield Magazine. October 1940.)*

*Ad (Courtesy of Outdoor Life Magazine. October 1923.)*

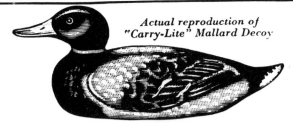

Actual reproduction of "Carry-Lite" Mallard Decoy

## THE DECOY YOU HAVE WAITED FOR!

The hollow-molded "CARRY-LITE" Decoy weighs less than 12 oz.; needs no weights for balance; can't tip or list; contains no "stuffing" to water-log if shot into; is completely water-proof; rights itself when tossed into water. Made slightly over-size, finished in natural duck colors... *mallard, canvas-back, blue-bill, pintail, drakes and hens.* Embossed feathers. Price: $9.75 per doz. (slightly higher west of Rockies.) See your dealer or send $1 direct for Sample Decoy.

**MOLDED CARRY-LITE DECOYS** 2603N. 30th St. Milwaukee, Wis.

*Ad (Courtesy of Field & Stream Magazine. November 1940.)*

*Wherever Ducks Fly...*
## CARRY-LITE DECOYS
have been bringing 'em in since 1939!

**Get Your Copy of Gordon MacQuarrie's Duck Hunters' Handbook**

Written for outdoor men by a real outdoor writer, packed with interesting and helpful information, drawn from the writer's broad experience and personal contacts. Send 25¢ for your copy of this fully illustrated, 56-page handbook . . . written especially for CARRY-LITE by one of your favorite outdoor authors. And don't forget your CARRY-LITE DECOYS.

First Light-Weight Decoy . . . First Choice Among Discriminating Sportsmen

**Sold By Leading Dealers Everywhere**

**CARRY-LITE DECOYS, Division Pulp Reproduction Co.**
3002 WEST CLARK STREET, MILWAUKEE 10, WISCONSIN

*Ad (Courtesy of Outdoor Life Magazine. October 1946.*

## Duck Days

Stools rigged...wings in the distance. If you outfitted at A & F, you're ready for them with a hard-hitting gun, the right decoys, correct ammunition... and comfortably warm clothes.

CARRY-LITE DUCK DECOY— extremely lifelike. Of light, water-proofed materials. Will not tip or list; no weights necessary for balance. $10 per dozen.

PORTABLE WALNUT GUN RACK—holds three guns. Nicely finished in genuine walnut. Easily attached to wall. $4.75.

Smith Shotguns . . . . . $49 to $1,327
Greener Guns . . . . $285 to $440
Francotte Imported Guns . . . $200 to $550

MADISON AVENUE at 45th STREET, NEW YORK

## ABERCROMBIE & FITCH CO.

*Even the renowned company of Albercrombie and Fitch offered Molded Carry-Lite decoys in 1940. Ad (Courtesy of Field & Stream Magazine. November 1940.)*

Don't Forget to Get
## CARRY-LITE
MOLDED DECOYS

Your water-fowl shooting equipment isn't complete without CARRY-LITE DECOYS. They're as light as 11 ounces of goose feathers; as water-proof as a new pair of rubbers; as natural appearing as the birds they attract. No weights needed for balance. Five types: MALLARD, BLUE-BILL, PINTAIL, CANVAS-BACK, BLACK DUCK drakes and hens. New, also, are the full-size GOOSE and MINIATURE DUCKS Also CROW and OWL Decoys for year round shooting. See them at your favorite sporting goods store. Write for full-color catalog sheet. **MOLDED CARRY-LITE DECOYS** 2603 No. 30th St., Milwaukee, Wis.

*Molded Carry-Lite also produced owl and crow decoys for year round shooting. Ad (Courtesy of Sports Afield Magazine. October 1941.)*

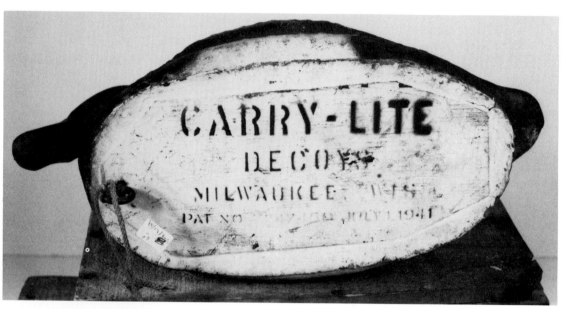

*Early bluebill decoy by Molded Carry-Lite c-1939. (Collection of Morton and Carol Kramer.)*

*Bottom of 1939 bluebill decoy showing stenciled name and address and patent date.*

*A hunter in Michigan readying his decoys for the upcoming waterfowl season in 1941. He is painting the bill on a Molded Carry-Lite decoy.*

*A molded Carry-Lite Canada goose that was made about 1946 - shown with the goose are molded representations of its favorite food made also by Molded Carry-Lite of Milwaukee, Wisconsin. (Collection of the author.)*

*A pair of Molded Carry-Lite Canada goose decoys made during the 1940's. Note the different physical characteristics between these birds and those of General Fibre Company. (Collection of the author.)*

*A pair of early Molded Carry-Lite canvasback decoys made in the 1940's, all original condition. (Collection of the author.)*

## JOSEPH COUDON

Joseph Coudon was a sportsman-artist who lived in Aikin in Cecil County, Maryland, a short distance north of Perryville, which was located on the shores of the famous Susquehanna Flats. Sometime before 1900 Mr. Coudon began manufacturing a folding rack consisting of three silhouette decoys. Mr. Coudon's artistic talent was readily apparent when the paint patterns on his silhouette decoys was displayed. Many of the decoys were stamped with the name COUDON AND CO. and the address AIKIN, MD. on them. They were made of one half inch white pine, some with their edges rounded off and others left with a sharp edge. The extra light decoys offered in their ad were made of a much thinner masonite like material. In the ad reproduced here the spelling of the name "COUDON" is incorrect and it can only be assumed that this was a type-setting error.

*Ad (Courtesy of The North-Western Sportsman. October 1905.)*

*J.Coudon & Company mallard silhouette decoy all original c-1890. (Collection of Dan Brown.)*

# JACOB DANZ, JR.

St. Paul, Minnesota

J. Danz, Jr. patented a tin profile duck decoy attached to a wooden bottom board on July 12, 1881 and a similar goose decoy on August 7, 1883. Little else is known of the company, but a number of the decoys manufactured have been discovered and added to collections. Elaborate paint feathering has added to the interest in collecting these decoys. Unfortunately the paint did not adhere well to the tin and many of the birds found today are missing a goodly portion of their original paint. The mallard drake pictured here from the collection of Dr. Morton Kramer is in excellent condition and displays very well the fine paint work. In an advertisement from *Forest and Stream Magazine,* it shows the folding silhouette decoy as having the profile of a duck on each side of the wooden bottom board. The one in the water to act as a keel when in use and also to prevent any problems of resetting the decoy should it turn over in rough water. The mallard in Dr. Kramer's collection has a regular tin keel. Although both the duck and goose decoy were patented in the name of Jacob Danz, apparently he formed a partnership with a Mr. Horne to manufacture and distribute the ducks. The ad included here from 1885 and a later ad in *Forest and Stream Magazine* dated 1889 show the name of the company as Horne and Danz, Sole Manufacturers, St. Paul, Minnesota. The ad in the 1889 issue of *Forest and Stream* lists Danz' patent folding decoys, ducks, geese, crane, pelican, swan. They also offered Danz patent minnow pails, "the best in the market."

*Danz mallard drake in near mint condition. Note the elaborate feathering patterns. (Collection of Morton and Carol Kramer.)*

*A Danz Company folding sheet metal silhouette Canada goose decoy photographed at Drum Point Farm on the Choptank River. These goose decoys were patented in 1883 and many of the examples in collections date from that period. (Collection of the author.)*

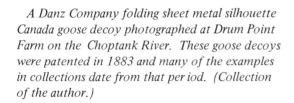

*Advertisement from an issue of <u>Forest and Stream</u> dated. 1885.*

*A rig of four Danz Decoy Company folding sheet metal goose decoys in original paint. (Collection of Bill Underwood.)*

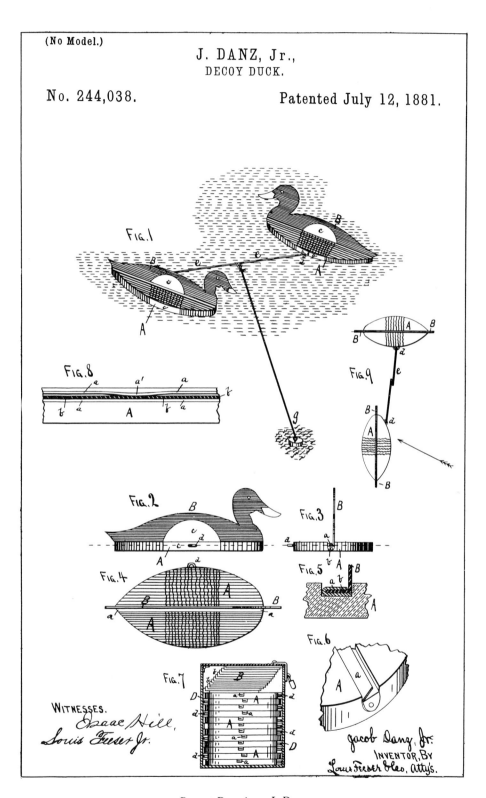

J. DANZ, Jr.,
DECOY DUCK.

No. 244,038.                    Patented July 12, 1881.

Patent Drawing - J. Danz.

## DEANCOYS
North Kansas City, Missouri

Deancoys first appeared in 1941 and were simple inflatable rubber decoys - made of a thin latex with color fast patterns developed in the rubber, they were inflated through an opening in the beak. Although they discontinued production due to the lack of materials during the war, they were back into operation and advertising decoys for sale in 1946. One would have to assume that a single piece of shot would render the Deancoy useless and yet their product was still being advertised in 1949.

Ad (Courtesy of Field & Stream Magazine. September 1942.

Ad (Courtesy of Sports Afield Magazine. October 1941.)

Ad (Courtesy of Outdoor Life Magazine. October 1943.)

## DEANCOYS

Mallard Deancoy in original condition. The bird
has a round patch type label affixed to the bottom
with the name and address of the manufacturer
imprinted on it. (Collection of the author.)

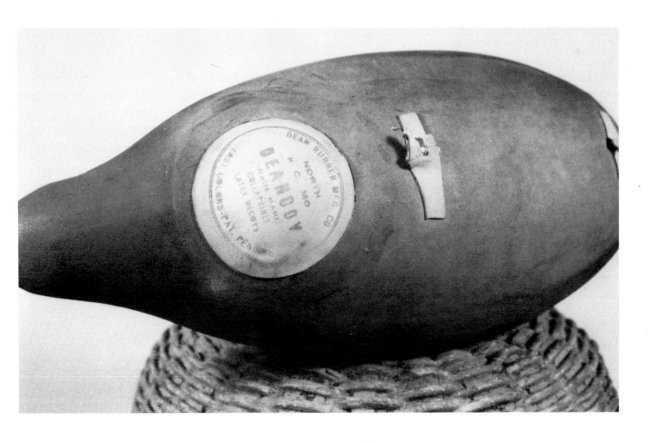

*Ad (Courtesy of Outdoor Life Magazine. November 1950.)*

## DEEKS, INC.

### Salt Lake City, Utah

Deeks were also inflatable latex rubber decoys with a molded cylinder shaped opening in the bottom. Into the lower edge of this cylinder opening was molded a round metal ring that acted as a balance weight when the bird was on the water. Although the idea seemed improbable to the author, when I dropped the pair here photographed onto the water, they instantly perked up into fully formed decoys. How effective they were under use seems debatable, but a number of hunters used them successfully in the 1940's and early1950's. Developed in 1941 they were still being advertised for sale in the November 1951 issue of *Outdoor Life Magazine*. There is an interesting photograph of Deeks decoys being demonstrated in a tin pail that has the name "DEEKS" imprinted on it in the book *Duck Decoys and How to Rig Them* by Ralf Coykendall published by Henry Holt in 1955. Apparently this pail was a salesman's aid and would be a nice addition to a factory decoy collectors paraphanelia.

*A pair of original Deeks mallard decoys made about 1950 and still functioning in good order. (Collection of the author.)*

*Ad (Courtesy of Field & Stream Magazine. October 1941)*

*Ad (Courtesy of Outdoor Life Magazine. November 1949)*

## DECOYS DELUX

Morrison, Illinois

These decoys were simply mounted mallards coated with a waterproofing material along their bottom edge and a hook for attaching a balance weight and an anchor line fastened in the proper locations to the bottom of the bird. This information and photo of a hen mallard is through the courtesy of Dr. Morton Kramer.

*Stuffed hen mallard offered for sale about 1939 by Decoys Delux.*

# DECOYS UNLIMITED

Erie, Pennsylvania

Jack Sweet began this decoy company in 1961 when requests for his hunting decoys were so frequent that he decided to go into business producing them. Jack had been hand carving decoys since the late 1940's and had become an accomplished decorative carver, when he decided to provide hunters with a good machine made wooden decoy. The bodies were made of hard balsa and the heads of white pine or cedar. Both were turned on duplicating lathes and sanded to a smooth finish. The heads were fitted with glass eyes. The paint work was rather fancy for hunting decoys and employed a lot of scratch combing and feathering. All of the birds were made somewhat oversized and were excellent hunting decoys. Many are still in use today on the Chesapeake Bay and, I am sure, other areas. For years Abercrombie and Fitch in New York City sold Jack Sweet's Decoys Unlimited birds and many of them are stenciled on the bottom "Made for Abercrombie and Fitch Co. by Decoys Unlimited."

*A rare white winged scoter made by Jack Sweet of Decoys Unlimited in Erie, Pennsylvania. This must have been a special order decoy done for someone who gunned along the coast. (Collection of Otto Johs.)*

*An excellent pair of Decoys Unlimited black ducks that were made for Abercrombie and Fitch in New York City - (Collection of the author.)*

*A pair of pintails in original paint by Decoys Unlimited of Erie, Pennsylvania, used for shooting pintails on the Chesapeake Bay. (Collection of the author.)*

FROM:
DECOYS UNLIMITED
R. D. #5
WATTSBURG ROAD
ERIE, PENNA.

## C.E. DELLENBARGER COMPANY

Joliet, Illinois

Absolutely no information was discovered on any Dellenbarger decoys. From the advertisement, it appears they were made in a couple of grades, hollow, in balsa or airwood, as they call it, and with glass eyes. Perhaps a collector somewhere has a Dellenbarger decoy or can shed some light on the existence of this company.

*Ad (Courtesy of Field & Stream Magazine. November 1935.)*

## DELMARVA DECOYS

Herndon, Virginia

A new company manufacturing V-board silhouettes on an idea revolutionized at least ninety years ago by another Chesapeake Bay area innovator. This outfit was formed in 1980 by Cliff Brown, his brother Chris, and Dave Ritter. The V-board components are presently turned out in

## FOSTER P. DOANE

Boston, Massachusetts

The only information available on this company is the advetisement reproduced here from National Sportsman Magazine, August 1929. Ted Harmon of Barnstable, 'Massachusetts has an inflatable rubber Canada goose of a very early vintage that could have been produced by this company.

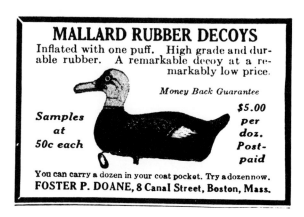
Virginia and assembled on Kent Island, the location of the earliest settlement in Maryland, and an area that possesses a rich waterfowling history. V-boards have been effectively employed in goose shooting on the Susquehanna Flats for many years.

*Canada goose V-boards or folding racks made by Delmarva Decoys of Herndon, Virginia. (Photo courtesy of Cliff Brown.)*

*White winged scoter V-board by Delmarva Decoys. (Photo courtesy of Cliff Brown.)*

# J.N. DODGE DECOY COMPANY

Detroit, Michigan

The J.N. Dodge Company began producing decoys in 1884 after purchasing the George Peterson decoy making venture and continued until 1894 when presumably, he went out of business. Enough has been published on the history of the big three decoy companies of Detroit that I will not go into any details here for fear of belaboring the facts. However an editorial comment, if I might be permitted, is in order as concerns the differentiation of Peterson, Dodge, and Mason decoys. It seems that all of the collectors of these beautiful machine made birds are completely unsure of who made which and it gets to the point where there is quite a bit of bickering, and in-fighting amongst those who are trying to discern the chronological order and correct attributions to be made in order to aid the Detroit factory decoy collector. Under the listing for each of these three factories in this book will be the barest of facts and a number of photographs of different or unusual specimens produced by each company. It is hoped that this will be sufficient for the purpose of this book. Harder facts and details can be found in John and Shirley Delphs' book *Factory Decoys,* in Cheever's *Mason Decoys,* in various periodicals on decoys, and in a new book to be released by Schiffer Publishing this year on Mississippi Flyway decoys written by Alan Haid.

J. N. DODGE,
276 and 278 Division street,        Detroit, Mich.

Manufacturer of Decoy Ducks of all kinds. First quality, $9 per doz.; second quality, $7: third quality, $5. Also geese, brant, coot, swan and snipe decoys. Duck and turkey calls. Decoys made like any pattern furnished, without extra charge. Large stock.

*Advertisement in Forest and Stream Magazine dated August 28, 1884.*

*An advertisement in Montgomery Ward's catalog of 1894-95 that depicts the exact same cut as in the Forest and Stream Magazine ad for J.N. Dodge. If this were an ad for Dodge decoys, it would be the last year they were produced and the price of $3.75 a dozen for the No. 1 best decoy ducks would be $5.25 a dozen less than when they were first offered in 1884 at $9.00 a dozen. The other ads for decoys in Ward's catalogs had distinctive cuts for each different kind of decoy offered which would lead one to assume that they were selling Dodge decoys here.*

I MAKE all kinds of Decoys of White Cedar, the lightest and most durable wood. I have constantly on hand all kinds of Duck Decoys, also Geese, Brant, Swan, Coot, Snipe and Plover Decoys; also the best Duck and Turkey Calls in the market. Decoys made after any model furnished without extra charge. Send for illustrated price list.

New Model No. 1 Mallard (Female).

St. Clair Flats or Sleeping Model of Male Red Head. When placed on water it is a perfect imitation of a Duck at rest and entirely unalarmed.

St. Clair Flats or Sleeping Model of Male Red Head.

**J. N. DODGE,**
278 Division Street,
DETROIT.

*J.N. Dodge advertisement from the back of W.B. Leffingwell's book Wildfowl Shooting published in 1888 by Rand McNally.*

*A mallard drake, No. 1 grade, in original paint by the J.N.Dodge Decoy Company. (Collection of the author.)*

*A rare Dodge hen canvasback in near mint condition. (Collection of Bill Butler.)*

*A J.N.Dodge Canada goose in excellent original condition and paint. (Collection of Bud Ward.)*

*J.N. Dodge Company Curlew in original paint-
(Courtesy Herbert Schiffer Antiques).*

*J.N.Dodge Company yellowleg decoy made in
Detroit Michigan. (Courtesy Herbert Schiffer Antiques.)*

*A rare Dodge Decoy Company swan - only a few
of these scarce decoys are known today. (Courtesy
Herbert Schiffer Antiques.)*

## SWAN-DOUGLAS DECOYS

Minneapolis, Minnesota

Information on this company again was limited to the advertisement reproduced here through the courtesy of *Sports Afield Magazine,* October 1940. Possibly the decoys were marked in some manner and someone may relate their bird to this ad.

*Ad (Courtesy of Sports Afield Magazine. October 1940.)*

*Ad (Courtesy of Outdoor Life Magazine. October 1946.)*

*This pair of Down East goldeneyes are in original paint and display well the natural attitude of these decoys. (Collection of Morton and Carol Kramer.)*

## DOWN EAST SPORTSCRAFT

Freeport, Maine

Details on the operations of this company have remained sketchy at best and attempts by the author to locate someone who could enlighten the decoy collecting world proved in vain. I will bet that information will come flowing from everywhere after this is published. The Down East birds seem to be considered valuable by their owners and when offered on the market, the price asked reflects this valuation. Perhaps the fact that Bill Mackey pictured two blackducks in his book, *American Bird Decoys,* accounts for some of their popularity. They were obviously turned on a duplicating lathe and left in that familiar rough feather finish, but the attitude and style was considerably greater than the "Pascagoula Decoys." The paint patterns were quite a bit more sophisticated also. They were made in hollow and solid models and had glass eyes inserted. Pintails, black ducks, mallards, and goldeneyes are known.

70

# DUCK-IN DECOY COMPANY

St. Louis, Missouri

These headless decoys were introduced to the sporting public in 1937 and seemed to have gained favor with waterfowl hunters everywhere. Quite a few have turned up and are in collections today. Made of excelsior filled cotton printed with a very nice pattern, they were used to simulate feeding ducks. They were offered in mallard, pintails, and black ducks.

High flyers, fast flyers...it makes no difference, this new headless decoy stops them! Ducks see Duck-Ins first — they're visible further, more attractive from the air. They're the surest way to more ducks this year!

If your dealer can't supply you, send $6.00 check or money order to Dept. C for 8 drakes and 4 hens, postpaid, complete with cords and anchors. Weight only 7 pounds. Order now!

**$6.00** per dozen complete

**D U C K - I N**
DECOY COMPANY
4060 Forest Park Blvd.
St. Louis, Mo.

*Ad (Courtesy of Hunting & Fishing Magazine. September 1937.)*

## DECOY MORE DUCKS!

High flyers, fast flyers . . . it makes no difference, this new headless decoy stops them! Ducks see Duck-Ins first. They're visible further, more attractive from the air. A sure way to more ducks this year.

Only $6.00 per dozen complete with cords and anchors.

Write today for illustrated literature. Please include your dealer's name.

**DUCK-IN DECOY COMPANY**
4065 Forest Park          St. Louis, Mo

*Ad (Courtesy of Fur-Fish-Game magazine. October 1937.)*

*A mint pair of black duck Duck-In decoys. (Collection of Morton and Carol Kramer.)*

*Mallard drake Duck-In decoy showing the fanciful paint pattern. (Collection of Dan Brown.)*

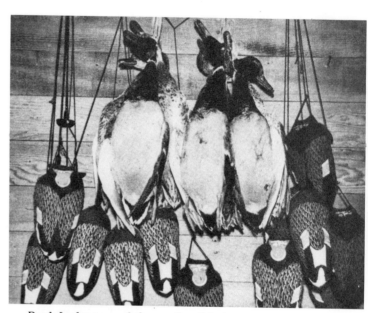

*Duck-In decoys and the results of their successful employment.*

## DUCKOYS

Oyster Bay, New York

Duckoys were apparently supplied unpainted and in a kit form so that the purchaser was responsible for assembling and painting the decoy. They were made of balsa wood and fitted with the best handmade glass eyes. Full color charts of the different species of ducks were furnished for the purpose of serving as a painting guide. They were priced at $16.50 per half dozen birds. Dates for this company have not been established. Their four page brochure displayed a hen and a drake for seven different species, mallard, black duck, pintail, canvasback, bluebill, red head, and goldeneye.

# DUCKOYS

## MAKE THE FINEST DECOYS IN THE WORLD

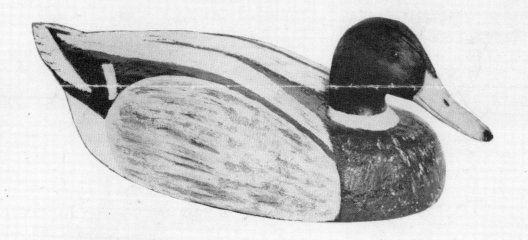

### *DYNA-MODEL PRODUCTS COMPANY*

76 SOUTH STREET, OYSTER BAY, NEW YORK

*The front cover of a four page brochure advertising Duckoys by Dyna-Model Products Company.*

# DUNSTER SPORTING GOODS COMPANY

## DUPE-A-GOOSE DECOYS

Seattle, Washington

Dunster Sporting Goods Company produced cardboard goose decoys that folded flat when not in use and spread open on a stake to form a full bodied decoy when employed in a field. They also manufactured similar floating goose decoys and floating Dupe-a-Duck decoys in mallard, pintail, black duck, scaup, and canvasback. The heads on the geese were riveted to the body and were movable so that they could be folded down into the body for protection when being carried back and forth to the hunting grounds. All of the cardboard decoys were heavily coated with wax for waterproofing. They were light, easy to handle, and effective under field conditions. Several of their ads are reproduced here to show the different ideas in advertising indicating their successfulness.

Ad (Courtesy of Fur-Fish-Game Magazine. November 1946.)

Ad (Courtesy of Outdoor Life Magazine. October 1945.)

# Good Hunting...

## with FOLDING
## DUPE-A-GOOSE DECOYS!

You can be sure of your share of *good* goose hunting this season when you use the life-like DUPE-A-GOOSE folding decoys. Hunters say "we bagged our limit in less than an hour and all credit is due to the DUPE-A-GOOSE decoys." Durable, yet light weight gives you the added advantage of carrying more Decoys with GREATER EASE. A flip of the spreader hinge and they become full bodied and ready to "bring them in" to you.

(Actual Photo of Decoys)
Upper: Regular stakeout in Canada, Snow, Specklebelly and Blue. Lower: Feeding . . . Canada only.

### Check These Advantages
● **Natural movement in the breeze**
● **Folds flat for easy carrying**
● **Sturdy . . . yet light in weight**

**$18.00 per dozen**

Order yours today at your sporting goods dealer or direct from factory . . . free folder on request.

### DUNSTER Sporting GOODS CO.
16824 PACIFIC HIGHWAY    SEATTLE 88, WASH.

*Ad (Courtesy of Outdoor Life Magazine. October 1950.)*

*Dunster "Dupe-a-Duck" cardboard mallard drake decoy, Seattle, Washington. c-1949. (Collection of the author.)*

*Dunster "Dupe-a-Goose" cardboard goose decoy, Seattle, Washington c-1949. (Collection of the author.)*

*Ad (Courtesy of Field & Stream Magazine. October 1947.)*

FOLDING
DUPE-A-DECOYS
Are
12 DECOYS IN EACH HAND

COMPACT
✓ CHECK THESE FEATURES
FULL BODIED WHEN SET
● Fold Flat          ● Natural Action
● Easy to Use     ● Tough Fibreboard

Send for FREE FOLDER

**FEEDING STAKEOUT GOOSE**
Adds naturalness to any decoy spread. Folds flat. Natural action in breeze. Species Canada, only.
DOZEN . . . . . $18.00
Each . . . . . . . . 1.75

**STAKEOUT GOOSE**
Built-in-Spreader. Socket-joint stake allows natural action in breeze. Species: Canada, Snow, Specklebelly, Blue.
DOZEN . . . . . . $18.00
Each . . . . . . . . . 1.75
Carrying Case . . . 2.50

Photo shows naturalness of DUPE-A-GOOSE spread using regular and feeding decoys.

**FLOATING GOOSE**
Designed for duck and goose hunter. Guaranteed to increase draw of any duck spread. Built-in-Balance. Folds Flat.
3 Decoys & Case $ 6.50
12 Decoys . . . . . . $18.00

**DUPE-A-DUCK**
Folding Decoy. light, compact. Built-in-Balance. natural action, non-tipping. In: Mallard, Pintail, Black Duck, Canvasback, Scaup.
12 Decoys, Case $11.95
Dozen . . . . . 8.95
Each . . . . . . . .75

AT YOUR DEALER OR SENT POSTPAID
Money Order or Check
Send for FREE Folder

### DUNSTER Sporting GOODS CO.
16824 PACIFIC HIGHWAY    SEATTLE 88, WASH.

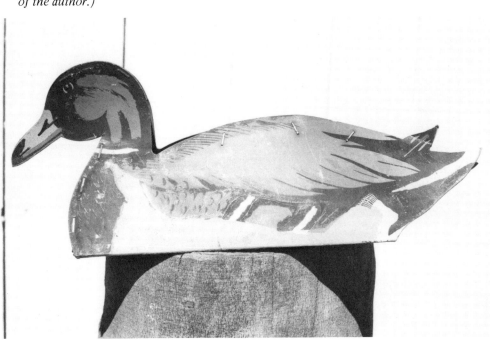

# EVANS DECOYS

Ladysmith, Wisconsin

Walter Evans began making decoys in the early 1920's with the help of an associate in Ladysmith, Wisconsin. History relates that a Mason premier mallard was his early inspiration. His decoys were made of local white cedar and turned one at a time on a duplicating lathe. He offered three grades of decoys, Mammoth, Standard, and Competitive. The Mammoth and standard grades could be had either solid or hollow bodied, while the Competitive was only offered as a solid decoy. The decoys were hollowed in the conventional Mason manner or with a one and one-quarter inch hole drilled through the breast into the body and then plugged. The Mammoth and Standard grade were smoothly finish sanded and the Competitive model was left with the feather finish circular lathe marks. All of the decoys were soaked in a mixture of white lead and oil and finish painted with white lead blended to the proper hue with base colors. This is one reason many Evans decoys are still found with outstanding original paint. Many of Walter Evans' decoys were rubber stamped "EVANS DECOY" on the bottom and this proves to be a sure fire identification mark.

Just as many others were produced and shipped without the rubber stamp. Walter Evans continued to produce decoys until about 1935 when, for reasons of ill health, he had to give up the business. Walter Evans was born in 1872 and died in 1948 at the age of 76.

*Walter Evans painting his decoys. Note the unique round, and probably revolving, painting bench. The racks alongside of him are full of what appear to be both Standard and Mammoth mallards and canvasbacks. Photo (Courtesy of Roger Ludwig.)*

*A pair of mint Mammoth grade Evans canvasbacks. (Collection of Les Brown.)*

*Original shipping label from the Evans Duck Decoy Company of Ladysmith, Wisconsin.*

FROM

# THE EVANS DUCK DECOY CO.

MANUFACTURERS OF

## LIKE-LIVE DUCK DECOYS

### LADYSMITH, WIS.

CONTENTS-FOURTH-CLASS MATTER-MERCHANDISE

POSTMASTER: This parcel may be opened for postal inspection if necessary

TO

A pair of standard Evans mallards. Note the simpler paint as compared to the Mammoth birds. (Collection of Morton and Carol Kramer.)

Evans Mammoth mallard pair. (Courtesy of Roger Ludwig.)

1931 retail price list circular by Evans Decoy Company. (Courtesy of Roger Ludwig and Walter Evans, Jr.)

1931                                    1932

## Price List

Manufactured by

## EVANS DUCK DECOY COMPANY

Ladysmith, Wisconsin

LIVE BIRDS ARE OUR MODELS

PERFECTION OUR AMBITION

The Evans Duck Decoys, both solid and hollow, are the finest and most natural that man can make. They are exact reproductions of the ducks they are intended to decoy.

They are made of select quality cedar especially treated to resist moisture and hand-painted with the highest grades of non-shine oil paints. Heads are hand carved and imported eyes are used to give them that natural appearance.

They are flat bottomed and float high in the water. Their perfect shape and true coloring account for their popularity. They will attract where other decoys fail.

These decoys are made in Mallards, Canvas-Backs, Blue Bills, Pin Tails, Blue and Creen Wing Teal, Red Heads and Coots.

All varieties are made in two sizes—mammoth and standard—in both solid and hollow.

ANY DUCK CAN FLY, BUT—

## Retail Price List

DEALER'S PRICE LIST ON REQUEST

|  | DOZEN |
|---|---|
| No. 10—MAMMOTH HOLLOW<br>Weight about 27 Lbs. per Doz. | $25.00 |
| No. 50—MAMMOTH SOLID -<br>Weight about 36 Lbs. per Doz. | $20.00 |
| No. 20—STANDARD HOLLOW<br>Weight about 18 Lbs. per Doz. | $14.00 |
| No. 1—STANDARD SOLID -<br>Weight about 23 Lbs. per Doz. | $12.50 |
| No. 1c—COMPETITIVE - -<br>Weight about 23 Lbs. per Doz. | $10.00 |

## Standard Packing

Eight Drakes, Four Hens to the Dozen.

All Prices F.O.B. Ladysmith, Wis.

IT TAKES THE EVANS DUCK TO DECOY

*Evans blue wing teal drake. (Courtesy of Roger Ludwig.)*

*Pair of Evans Competitive grade mallards. Note the circular blade marks left on as a rough feather finish -(courtesy of Roger Ludwig.)*

*Pair of Evans Standard bluebills - (Courtesy of Roger Ludwig.)*

*A pair of Evans Standard grade canvasbacks (Courtesy of Roger Ludwig.)*

*Standard and Mammoth grade pintail drakes by Evans Decoy Company. (Courtesy of Roger Ludwig.)*

*A pair of Standard grade Evans redheads. (Courtesy of Roger Ludwig.)*

*A pair of Evans Competitive grade bluebills showing the rough feather finish. (Courtesy of Roger Ludwig.)*

*A pair of Mammoth grade Evans bluebills with a much more elaborate paint style than that of the Standard grade bluebills. (Courtesy of Roger Ludwig.)*

*An Evans Decoy Company American coot in original paint and condition. (Collection of the author.)*

*Evans Decoy Company standard grade mallards. (Courtesy of Roger Ludwig.)*

## E—Z MANUFACTURING COMPANY

East Dedham, Massachusetts

Another inflatable rubber decoy about which very little is known. The cut in the one ad is distinctive enough that someone might possibly recognize a rubber decoy that they own. The company possibly started in 1932.

*Ad (Courtesy of Field & Stream Magazine. November 1935.)*

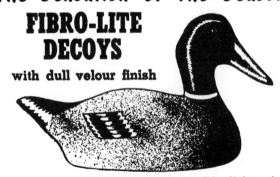

*Ad (Courtesy of Sports Afield Magazine. November 1940.)*

*Ad (Courtesy of Sports Afield Magazine. October 1941.)*

## FIBRO-LITE PRODUCTS COMPANY

Minneapolis, Minnesota

A new decoy in 1940, Fibro—Lite Decoys have yet to be identified by the collector. apparently another paper composition decoy, they were probably in operation until the beginning of World War II and then ran into stiff competition after the war from manufacturers of similar material birds such as General Fibre, Carry-Lite, and Animal Trap Company of America.

*Ad (Courtesy of National Sportsman Magazine. November 1936.)*

84

# FLAP-O-MATIC

The Flap-O-Matic decoy was a molded hard rubber bird with a lot of detail in the molding and a painstakingly fine paint job. The wings were separate and hinged and attached to the back of the decoy in such a manner that when pulled by a string the wings opened and appeared to be flapping. The birds had to be anchored securely before pulling the string to flap the wings could be accomplished. The little information available such as the name and location of the manufacturer was molded into the keel on the decoy.

*Hen mallard decoy by Flap-O-Matic Company. (Collection of Morton and Carol Kramer.)*

*Drake mallard decoy by Flap-O-Matic. (Collection of the author.)*

## FLYWAY DECOYS

### Wading River New Jersey

Bob and Lyn Jones of Washington Township in Burlington County, New Jersey operate one of the last four commercial wooden decoy manufacturering enterprises. They have a sixteen spindle duplicating lathe in their small factory which is located in a rural section of the New Jersey pine barrens. The Jones have been producing wooden decoys there under the name "Flyway Decoys" for over eight years and have built up a tremendous mail order business, shipping their birds all over the United States. Their decoys are made of sugar pine, fitted with glass eyes, and sold painted or unpainted. A large rig of these wooden birds were hunted over at the Castle Haven Gun Club in Dorchester County, Maryland.

*Bob Jones working the lathe in his decoy factory. His machine can turn out sixteen decoys at a time.*

*Bob Jones of Flyway Decoys standing among the racks of his unfinished decoys.*

86

# FOLDUCK DECOYS

Broken Bow, Nebraska

FOLDUCK Decoys—Folding Duck Decoys, waterproof canvas body, compact, light to carry, good floaters. Low price. Write for Free Folder. Send 9c stamps for booklet "Decoy Setting." Folduck Decoys, Broken Bow, Nebraska.

*Classified advertisement in October 1941 issue of Hunting and Fishing Magazine.*

# G & H GOOSE DECOY COMPANY

Henryetta, Oklahoma

The author has a similar appearing goose decoy made of a thin molded paper composition shell. The bird has no markings but from the photo in the ad pictured here, they could be one and the same.

THE hollow Goose Decoys pictured above are made up in full size Canadian Honkers and Snow Geese, with short or long head, sold separate or assorted. These decoys are field type.

Pictured below shows the same Decoys knocked down for convenience in carrying, six decoys to a package, weighing only 6½ pounds per dozen.

These Decoys have been on the market for the past 9 years and have proven satisfactory to all hunters who have used them. For further information write us for pamphlet.

NO DEALERS THIS YEAR. ORDER DIRECT.

**PRICE $18.50 per DOZEN, plus SALES TAX**

**F.O.B. HENRYETTA, OKLAHOMA**

**G.&H. GOOSE DECOY**

**COMPANY**

**Box 937**

**Henryetta, Oklahoma**

*Ad (Courtesy of Outdoor Life Magazine. November 1948.)*

# GENERAL FIBRE COMPANY

St. Louis, Missouri

General Fibre Company began producing paper mache decoys after World War II entering the field against the already established molded Carry-Lite Company and the Animal Trap Company paper decoys. They made seven different species of ducks, Canada geese, and a crow shooters kit consisting of a fibre owl and two fibre crow decoys. Their birds were manufactured under the brand name of "Ariduck." The fact that this company produced these paper composition decoys all through the 1950's and into the early 1960's accounts for the numerous examples of their work that are found today.

**ARIDUK BRINGS 'EM IN**

Birds of a feather flock together . . . that's why the naturalness and "relaxed" design of ARIDUK Decoys "attract". Their Fibre construction is lightweight yet durable. For ducks, geese or crows . . . ARIDUK lures down the game.

**ARIDUK Duck Decoys**

Seven realistic species . . . won't sink when shot into or lose shape in use; waterproof with no seam bottom, self-righting, anchor hooks installed.

**ARIDUK Goose Decoy**

Exact replica of Canadian Goose, two models, shell for field hunting, full body for both field and stream. Stakes supplied, anchor hooks installed. Removable feeder and straight necks for both models.

**Crow-Shooter's Kits**

Hunter's choice of Great Horned Owl with Crow Decoys or Two-Face Owl with Crow Decoys . . . great for thrilling all year around shooting.

Write for Free Catalog . . . Dept. O

**GENERAL FIBRE COMPANY**

**1723 Locust St. • St. Louis 3, Mo.**

*Ad (Courtesy of Outdoor Life Magazine. November 1955.)*

*A crow shooter setting his rig of General Fibre Company crow decoys in March of 1949.*

*A group of Ariduck molded paper composition goose decoys made by the General Fibre Company of St. Louis, Missouri. Made about 1955-60. (Collection of the author.)*

*Ad (Courtesy of Field & Stream Magazine. October 1958.)*

*General Fibre Company molded Canada goose decoys - standard size in the foreground and over-size in the back. (Collection of the author.)*

## GUNDELFINGER WOOD

## PRODUCTS COMPANY

Jefferson City, Missouri

Gundelfinger Decoys were made during the second half of the 1920's by the company that was the successor to the J.M. Hays Wood Products Company also of Jefferson City, Missouri. Manufactured under the trademark *"Ducklures,"* Gundelfinger Decoys are hardly discernible from many of the other wooden birds produced throughout the Mississippi Flyway on duplicating lathes. They were left in the feather finish showing the lathe marks, were hollow Idaho cedar, and were fitted with glass eyes. Their ad states that they offered decoys in 1928 in thirteen different species. They also made an "all wood" collapsible decoy of northern white pine. Fully painted with glass eyes, they folded into a light weight, compact, easy to carry decoy when not in use. *Hunting and Fishing Magazine,* for several years in the late 1920's, offered Gundelfinger Decoys as a premium for selling a predescribed number of subscriptions to their magazine.

**Gundelfinger's "All Wood" COLLAPSI-BLE DUCK DECOYS.** By a fortunate pur-chase we are able to offer our subscription agents 1 dozen of these excellent life-like de-coys as a prize for only **6 new subscriptions at $1.00 each.**

*Ad (Courtesy of Hunting and Fishing Magazine. July 1930.)*

*Ad (Courtesy of Field & Stream Magazine. November 1927.)*

*Ad (Courtesy of Hunting and Fishing Magazine. November 1928.)*

Gundelfinger's "All-Wood" Collapsible Decoys, made entirely of selected Northern white pine. Fold flat, very light in weight, float upright under all conditions, life like painting of various specie. One dozen of these excellent decoys given as a prize for 12 new subscriptions at $1.00 each. Mention specie wanted when ordering.

*Ad (Courtesy of Hunting and Fishing Magazine. November 1928)*

Gundelfinger's Famous "Superior" hollow duck decoys of genuine Idaho cedar, hand painted, life size, glass eyes, feather finish. Name specie desired when ordering. One dozen of these decoys given as a prize for 20 new subscriptions at $1.00 each.

*Ad (Courtesy of Hunting and Fishing Magazine. November 1928.)*

Gundelfinger's "All Wood" COLLAPSIBLE DUCK DECOYS. By a fortunate purchase we are able to offer our subscription agents 1 dozen of these excellent life-like decoys as a prize for only 6 new subscriptions at $1.00 each.

*Ad (Courtesy of Hunting and Fishing Magazine. December 1930.)*

# H.L. HAMMAN DECOYS

Middletown, Delaware

Excellent cork hunting decoys with pine heads and thin plywood bottom boards. These decoys are used extensively on the Delmarva Penninsula and are made locally by a hunter, H.L. Hamman in Middletown, Delaware.

*A Canada goose and black duck decoy made of cork by H. L. Hamman.*
*(Collection of the author.)*

*A like new mallard drake by H.L.Hamman of Middletown, Delaware. All of these cork birds are made oversized. (Collection of the author.)*

## DECOYS & CALLERS

*Ad (Courtesy of National Sportsman Magazine. October 1936.)*

*Ad (Courtesy of Outdoor Life Magazine. October 1938.)*

## HANSELLS CORK DECOYS

Gopher Sports Supply Company

Minneapolis, Minnesota

Nothing is known of these decoys and it is doubtful if any have ever been identified. From the cut in the ad they appear similar to several other makes of cork decoys, so unless they might possibly have been marked in some manner, we may never delineate this factory bird.

## KEN HARRIS

Woodville, New York

Ken Harris has made fine hunting decoys and decoratives in his shop in Woodville, New York since the mid 1930's. The Harris decoys, whether hunting birds or decoratives, have outstanding paint patterns applied by Mr. Harris and one of his assistants, Sterling O'Yong. He produced decoys out of both northern white pine and hard grain balsa and they were usually stenciled on the bottom with *Ken Harris, Woodville, N.Y.* Photos of Mr. Ken Harris and his helpers appear in Hal Sorenson's January, February, March 1965 issue of *The Decoy Collectors Guide.*

*Wood duck decoy by Ken Harris, Woodville, New York - 1950's. (Collection of Bill Butler.)*

*A Ken Harris gunning model black duck decoy - note the heavy comb painting on the back and head of this bird. Made c-1950. (Collection of the author.)*

*A Ken Harris drake blue wing teal in excellent original paint. (Collection of the author.)*

## J.M. HAYS WOOD PRODUCTS COMPANY

Jefferson City, Missouri

The J.M. Hays Wood Products Company started manufacturing wooden decoys sometime around 1920 in Jefferson City, Missouri. It is only conjecture at this point, but it appears that the company either began as, or bought out, Benz "Lifelike" Decoys also of Jefferson City. The Hays decoys for years have confused collectors of Mason decoys, because of their almost identical physical conformation and paint patterns. It is certain that Hays or Benz, whichever came first, was strongly influenced by the Mason birds. They couldn't have picked a better decoy to copy. J.M. Hays offered the waterfowl hunter two models, the slightly oversized hollow "Grand Prix" with the fancy paint job and the solid standard sized "Superior" model with the less sophisticated paint patterns. They advertised as being the only wood working plant in the world with its own lakes on which they raised mallards to be used as live models for their decoys. In their 1922 catalog, they had eighteen different species of ducks listed for which they made decoys. Whether or not all of these were ever made or not remains to be seen. They also listed steel profiles for Canada geese, Wilson's snipe, and brant. A number of excellent original paint Hays teal decoys can be found in the collection at Shelburne Museum. The Hays decoy ballast weights had a key with the name and address on either side impressed into the leads. The 1921 ad in *Outdoor Life Magazine* shows this identifying mark as being on each decoy.

*Ad (Courtesy of Outdoor Life Magazine. October 1923.)*

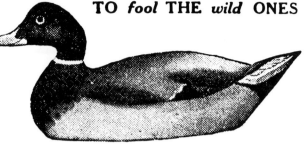

Ad (Courtesy of Outdoor Life Magazine.
April 1921.)

Ad (Courtesy of Outdoor Life Magazine.
October 1921.)

*J.M.Hays mallard drake. Note the strikingly similar conformation and paint to a Mason Premier mallard. (Collection of Tom Witte.)*

*Rare Animal Trap Company of Mississippi baldpate decoy - in mint original condition with the round Animal Trap Company rubber stamp on the bottom.*

*Victor Animal Trap blue wing teal in original condition. The head was originally left free on this decoy so that it could be turned to any position when rigged out, while the head on the preceding baldpate was originally glued turned to the left.*

*Victor D-9 tentite mallard decoy first offered by the Animal Trap Company of America at Lititz, Pennsylvania.*

*Three stuffed canvas decoys, two mallard drakes and a pintail drake made by the Armstrong Featherweight Decoy Company of Houston, Texas.*

*A pair of mallard silhouettes from a folding rack made by J. Coudon & Company of Aikin, Maryland, c.-1890. These two birds illustrate the outstanding paint work that was applied to the Coudon V-boards.*

*A V-board rack of blackhead or scaup silhouettes by Joseph Coudon of Aikin, Maryland, c-1900-1910.*

*A very rare original paint bufflehead drake by the J.N. Dodge Company of Detroit, Michigan, c-1890's.*

*A page from a 1930's color catalog from the J.M. Hays Decoy Company showing the redhead and green wing teal decoys they had for sale.*

A Down East Decoy Company solid body sleeping mallard drake. These decoys were made in Portland, Maine by the Coffin Brothers and were offered in both solid and hollow models.

An early J.N. Dodge oversize mallard decoy in original condition made during the late 1880's. These large prime birds are seldom found in this condition.

A Herter's hollow black duck decoy made during the early 1930's, these fully carved birds are the premier examples of the many varieties of decoys made and offered by Herter's, Inc. of Waseca, Minnesota.

A Canada goose decoy by Herter's that is similar in period and design to the preceding black duck decoy. In fine original condition, this decoy is one of the more collectible items offered by the Herter's Company.

A pair of bluebill or scaup decoys made of balsa wood and in original paint - made by Herter's, Inc. after World War II.

A "Detroit" grade Mason black duck decoy with the scarce "BARRON" brand. This bird came out of the "BARRON" rig and was found on the Eastern Shore of Virginia where that club was located.

A Chesapeake Bay Model canvasback drake by the Mason Decoy Factory of Detroit, Michigan. A special model offered by Mason these birds were oversized and had higher heads than their normal canvasback decoys.

An exceptional pair or original paint glass eye 3rd grade or "Detroit" mallards by the Mason Decoy Factory of Detroit, Michigan.

A pair of Premier hollow blue wing teal by Mason Decoy Company of Detroit, Michigan. In almost mint condition, this is a truly outstanding pair of birds.

Two mallard drakes by the Mason Decoy Company. The front bird is a mint standard sized Challenge grade and the bird in the rear is a mammoth oversized special order Mason mallard.

A rare oversized Premier grade Mason white winged scoter. Decoys such as this fine piece were special orders by Mason and different examples continue to turn up as decoys are searched out by more and more collectors.

Another rare and possibly unique Mason special order decoy. Greatly oversized, this bird was one of fifty that were made for the False Cape Gun Club on Back Bay in Virginia. It has the "F.C.G.C." brand in the bottom and is in original condition. Found to be too large and unwieldy for gunning, they were seldom used and were washed away and lost from their boat shed on stilts during the fierce hurricane that struck the mid-Atlantic coast in 1933. This mallard is declared to be the only one of the original fifty left in existence today.

Mason Premier white wing scoter drake. This hollow Mason scoter was once in the rig of the Muskeget Gun Club on Nantucket.

A William E. Pratt Company blue wing teal drake. The "feather finish" on this nice little teal does not take away from the original paint.

William E. Pratt Company coot decoy in original paint.

A pair of balsa Al Ries "Tru-Dux" mallard decoys from Chicago, Illinois, almost mint condition, made c-1939-41.

A pair of pintails and a mallard drake made and offered by Sears Roebuck and Company under the brand name of J.C. Higgins. These paper mache birds are all original and were made during the 1950's.

Tuveson cedars - a pair of mallard decoys by the Tuveson Manufacturing Company of St. James, Minnesota, made c-1930.

Wildfowler Company black ducks - a standard size Quogue Wildfowler black duck in the foreground and a mammoth Point Pleasant Wildfowler black duck in the back. This huge bird was a special order model made with a black duck head on a hollow goose body.

Point Pleasant Wildfowler green wing teal drake-hollow body - from Charles Birdsall's personal rig.

A pair of fine original condition Old Saybrook Wildfowler widgeon. Made for and used by the Orville Reed Right Gun Club on Back Bay, Virginia. Note the brand "ORR" on the back of the birds.

Early hollow pine Old Saybrook Wildfowler canvasback drake in all original condition. Made c-1939 by Ted Mulliken.

Decorative model green wing and blue wing teal drakes - made about 1946 by Ted Mulliken at the Old Saybrook, Connecticut Wildfowler Company.

An excellent pair of Quogue Wildfowler mallards - the hen is the tucked head sleeper model. Fewer Wildfowler decoys were made at the Quogue, Long Island factory than at any of the other locations.

Unknown stuffed canvas hen pintail. Thought to have been made west of the Mississippi River - in excellent original condition.

A rare and possibly unique Stevens coot made in Weedsport, New York before 1890. This is the only Stevens coot known as of this writing.

Unknown factory mallard in original paint. The head on this bird releases by a spring and swings all the way down under the bird so that the bill tucks up into a slot cut in the bottom of the duck for that purpose. This decoy was hunted over in Kansas in the early twenties.

An almost mint Harvey Stevens pintail drake, Weedsport, New York, c-1880.

A pair of Quogue Wildfowler pintails in fine original condition. Both of these birds have the Quogue Wildfowler brand on the bottom.

Mallard drake by J.W. Reynolds Company of Chicago, Illinois. Note the similarity of carving design to any number of factory decoys, yet with a much finer paint style.

Fine original paint ruddy turnstone by Strater and Sohier of Boston, Massachusetts.

Three folding tin snipe decoys in original paint by Strater and Sohier of Boston, Massachusetts. Tin birds like these were patented in 1874.

Black duck decoys by the Wildfowler Company of Old Saybrook, Connecticut. This photo illustrates the three different head positions that Wildfowler offered, the tucked head, the normal position, and the high or alert head.

Four rare original paint merganser decoys by the William E. Pratt Company of Chicago, Illinois. These birds were found in New Hampshire, but originally hunted at Barnstable, Massachusetts on Cape Cod.

A pair of better grade Pratt mallards - smoothly finish sanded and with a fancier paint job, these Pratts were the top of the line.

*Redhead decoys made by the Wildfowler Company Old Saybrook, Connecticut, c-1946.*

*A mint original condition Dodge mallard. This bird has tack eyes and an especially nice paint job even though it was a lower grade of decoy offered by J.N. Dodge.*

*A rig mate to the preceding bird, this J.N. Dodge black duck decoy is in like condition.*

A No. 1 grade William E. Pratt Company goldeneye drake in smooth finish and original paint. Pratt decoys such as this were the finest offered by that company.

Factory black duck in the manner of Elmer Crowell - believed to have been made by a New England decoy company that used an Elmer Crowell black duck as a prototype. Left in the rough feather finish and nicely painted.

A rare and here-to-fore unknown pair of Mason "SNUGGLED HEAD" sleeper mallards in original paint. (Collection of Dave Afton).

# HERTER'S

Waseca, Minnesota

The Herter's Company produced many different models of decoys through the years. They started in business before 1900 and still offer styrofoam and plastic decoys today. Their early hollow cedar decoys with the rich wing and feather carving are eagerly sought by collectors of decoys and are quite valuable. At different periods of time they manufactured many varieties of birds in a number of different materials. Most of their models are photographed here.

*Ad (Courtesy of Sports Afield Magazine.)*

*Ad (Courtesy of Hunting and Fishing Magazine. October 1940.)*

*Herter's, Inc. of Waseca, Minnesota made balsa crows like this bird during the 1940's and the 1950's. (Collection of the author.)*

Common eider decoy made by Herter's, Inc. of Waseca, Minnesota. These birds were made into the 1960's. (Collection of the author.)

A pair of Herter's balsa coot decoys, one with a bottom board and one without. (Collection of the author.)

*A very nice balsa goldeneye drake made by Herter's, Inc. in about 1946 - original condition. (Collection of the author.)*

*Herter's balsa model canvasback with a tenite or plastic head. These decoys were introduced in the early 1950's. (Collection of the author.)*

*Herter's Santa Marta balsa field goose - full bodied with a feeding head, about 1946. (Collection of Ron Gard.)*

*Herter's black duck - cork body with a printed canvas cover and a machine carved pine head. These birds are thought to have been made around 1930-1940. (Collection of the author.)*

A small Herter's bluebill, just ten inches long and two inches thick. This bird is made of balsa with a pine head that is nicely done. Made just after World War II. (Collection of the author.)

A late red breasted merganser made by Herter's in about 1960. (Collection of the author.)

*Three solid wood mallard drakes by Herter's,
Inc. of Waseca, Minnesota. (Collection of the author.)*

*Hen mallard with a feeding or swimming head.
This bird is made of printed canvas over cork with
a wooden bottom board and head, c-1930's and
c-1940's. (Collection of Morton and Carol Kramer.)*

*Early hollow Herter mallards heavily carved and
beautifully painted, decoys of this quality are rare
and valuable - c-1920's and 1930's. (Collection
of Bobby Richardson.)*

## W.C. HUGGINS

Kansas City, Missouri

*An early rubber collapsible decoy duck. Ad (Courtesy of Field & Stream. August 1923.)*

*Ad (Courtesy of Outdoor Life Magazine. October 1931) The Ideal Decoy is also advertised for sale in the 1936 Wm. E. Pratt catalog. This explains the statement in the above advertisement that they were also available at their Illinois factory.*

## IDEAL DECOY COMPANY

Klamath Falls, Oregon

Advertised as hollow metal decoys that nested together includes the Ideal decoy as one of a number of hollow metal birds that were manufactured on the West Coast. It seems that tin was one of the more popular materials for decoys produced on the Pacific Coast. The Ideal decoy was advertised in 1931, but the "Anderson" and a very similar "Baker" hollow tin decoy were much earlier. A later product was the Chris Decoy Company located at 2520 Broadway in Sacramento, California. These decoys were also of the hollow, stamped out models that nested together. They had a mechanically printed rather than painted feather finish. One wonders as to the popularity of the metal decoy out west.

## JACKSON INDUSTRIES

Kalamazoo, Michigan

Marshall Jackson, 1898-1978, was a noted inventor from the Kalamazoo area and one of his inventions was the collapsible canvas Canada goose decoy pictured here. He manufactured these decoys for ten years from 1946 to 1956 and sold them through his sporting goods store in Kalamazoo. They were also carried by Marshall Fields in Chicago and Northside Hardware in Nebraska. The birds consisted of a silk screened canvas covering over a collapsible inner wire frame-work. They were made as field decoys and had a metal stake which passed through the center of the breast to the tail and supported them upright in the field. They had alert or feeding heads made of 3/4 inch white pine. A kit consisted of six decoys, stakes, and a canvas carrying case which sold for $18.00. The information and photographs on the Jackson decoys are through the courtesy of Ron Kurzman and Joe Johnson of Michigan.

*Jackson Industries Canada goose decoy in the field ready for use. (Collection of Ron Kurzman.)*

*Jackson Industries Canada goose decoy disassembled.*

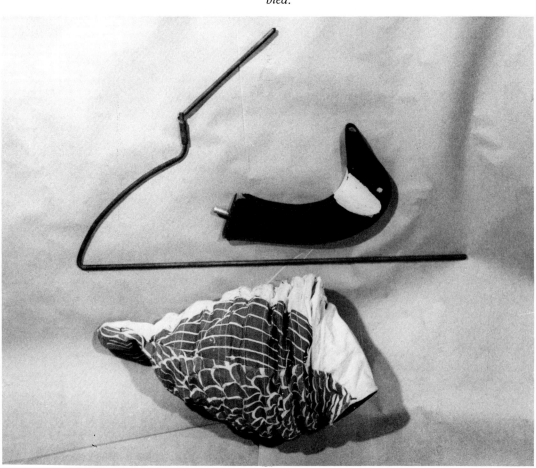

# WM. R. JOHNSON COMPANY

Seattle, Washington

Johnson's Folding Decoys, as they were originally known, were made of a heavy waterproofed cardboard or fibreboard with a photographic reproduction of a species of duck or goose imprinted on it. They were made with a wooden bottom board that slid into the bottom when the cardboard halves were spread for use as floaters on the water and with a metal stake to be used as stick-up field decoys. They folded flat when not in use and were light and easy to carry. Many goose hunters even today do not realize the effectiveness of silhouette decoys for use in fields or on the water. Tens of thousands of silhouette decoys are used successfully on the Eastern Shore of Maryland and these Johnson cardboard decoys were the progressive forerunners of today's silhouettes.

*Ad (Courtesy of Outdoor Life Magazine. November 1955.)*

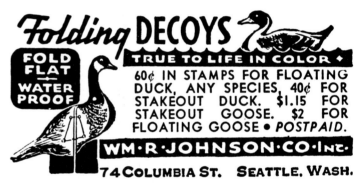

*Ad (Courtesy of Hunting and Fishing Magazine. October 1941.)*

*Ad (Courtesy of Field & Stream Magazine. October 1923.)*

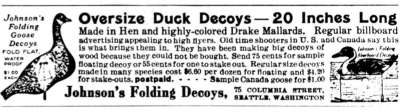

*Ad (Courtesy of Outdoor Life Magazine. October 1925.)*

**Stake-Out Decoys Weigh 4 Ozs., Cost 35c**
For Shallow Water and Field Shooting. Photographic reproductions of many kinds of ducks died out of heavy waterproof fiberboard. Bodies spread by inserting metal frame with wire leg attached. Also floating decoys weighing one-half pound each at 55 cents each, and oversize Canada stake-out goose at $1.00 each, sent postpaid on receipt of price Send 35c for Sample Postpaid **Johnson's Folding Decoys,** 75 COLUMBIA STREET, SEATTLE, WASHINGTON

*Ad (Courtesy of Outdoor Life Magazine. September 1925.)*

121

*Wm. R. Johnson hen mallard decoy. (Collection of Dan Brown.)*

*Canada goose decoy manufactured by Wm. R. Johnson of Seattle. ( Collection of Morton and Carol Kramer.)*

*A goose hunter in Montana in 1927 employing his Johnson's Folding goose decoys.*

*Bluebill decoy by Johnson's Folding Decoys displayed with the canvas carrying bags that were supplied with the decoys. (Collection of Morton and Carol Kramer.)*

*Bottom of the hen mallard decoy showing the printed advertisement. A curious notation on the Johnson Company: their various ads show them located at one time or another at No. 72, 74, 75, and 76 Columbia Street in Seattle, Washington.*

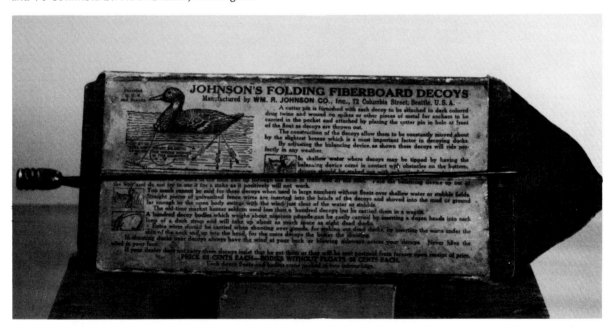

123

# K-D DECOY

Specialty Manufacturing Company

St. Paul, Minnesota

The Knockdown decoy was just that, a bird whose head came off and tucked into a head shaped cut-out inletted into the bottom of the body. The anchor cord was wound around the anchor weight and the weight then slid into slots cut so that once the lead was in place, it held the head into its cut-out. The body itself was made of a two inch thick piece of pine so that when the head and weight were in place, a compact little knock down decoy was the result. Undersized to begin with, the decoys probably didn't show well in big open water, but were a lot more effective on small ponds or creeks. The head of the bird was attached to the opposite end of the anchor cord which passed through a hole in the front of the body. When the anchor cord was pulled through the hole, the head popped right into its proper location and remained there as long as the line was somewhat taut. A rather ingenious idea, the K-D mallard decoys pictured with their original wooden box in which one dozen of them were shipped were purchased around 1920 in North Dakota and used there for hunting waterfowl. A number of different species have been located, but the mallard K-D decoy seems to be the most abundant.

*A pair of K-D decoys with the original box in which one dozen decoys were shipped. (Private collection.)*

*Another model K-D mallard with rounded and more finished head carving. (Collection of Morton and Carol Kramer.)*

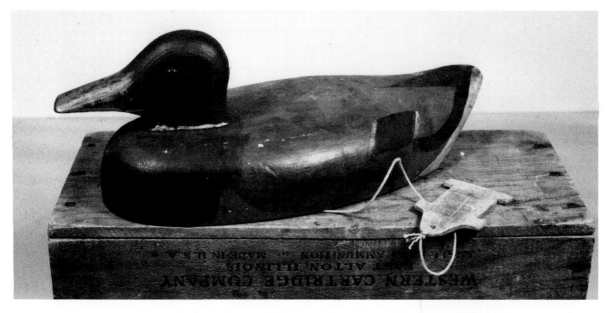

*A pair of mallard K-D decoys showing the drake ready for use and the hen with its head and weight stashed for carrying. (Collection of Dan Brown.)*

## MAJESTIC MOLDING COMPANY

Elyria, Ohio

A molded tenite decoy developed as an outgrowth of World War II. It is doubtful that such a company as Majestic Molding did much business at $54.00 a dozen for their decoys, when the duck hunter could go to old reliable Herter's the same year and get a dozen decoys for $24.00.

*Ad (Courtesy of Field & Stream Magazine. August 1947.)*

# MASON'S DECOY FACTORY

Detroit, Michigan

Mason's Decoy Factory is perhaps the most well known maker of commercial decoys. Almost every collector whose imagination has been entrapped by the fascination of the wooden decoy has heard of the Mason birds. Without a doubt they are more popular among collectors than any of the other factory decoys known. Their popularity is constantly reflected by the ever increasing prices that fine examples bring in today's decoy market. As has been said by many, there is nothing fancy or outstanding in the carving or conformation of Mason decoys; although a glimpse of a "snaky head" black duck, a "tucked head" snuggling redhead, or a certain long and slinky premier drake pintail at the Shelburne Museum might give rise to a more than mild discussion on that point. However, the true beauty and desirability of the Mason decoys is captured in the paint patterns that must have been applied with more attention and detail than most of us stop and give a thought to today. The blending of the colors, the design of the patterns, and the spattering, stippling, dotting, and streaking of backs and breasts all seemed to be a very important part of the painting process. We all loudly acclaim the painters of these decoys who gave us a finished product that affords so much pleasure to behold as they perch upon our shelves as though they were kings upon their thrones. No one can deny that an old repainted Mason goldeneye decoy is a very ordinary bird and a premier in that condition might bring $100.00 on today's market. Yet that same bird in good original paint displaying the dramatic color contrasts of the drake or the subtle feathering of the hen might bring fifteen times that amount. Taken together as a whole, with the fine stylish carving of some of the models and the muted sophisticated colorings of the aged original paint, Mason decoys have lured many a collector into their fold. The Mason's Decoy Factory started manufacturing decoys in 1896 and ceased production in 1924. History related that their patterns and equipment were purchased then by the Wm. E. Pratt Decoy Company and later passed to the Animal Trap Company of America when that company bought out Pratt in 1939. Mason's must have turned out many thousands of decoys during the twenty-eight years they were in business because hundreds of their birds continue to turn up today. Few of us mind that a good Mason decoy can still be found on a regular basis.

*A Mason Detroit grade American merganser decoy. (Collection of Morton and Carol Kramer.)*

*Hollow Mason Premier black duck in excellent original condition. (Collection of the author.)*

*Rare "Back Bay" model Mason redhead hen in original paint. These Back Bay decoys are almost never found in original paint as the hunters in that region tended to repaint their decoys every year. (Collection of Morton and Carol Kramer.)*

*Mason swan in the collection of the Refuge Water-fowl Museum in Chincoteague, Virginia. At one time this bird was mounted on the roof of a Back Bay gun club. Photo (Courtesy of The Refuge Waterfowl Museum - Chincoteague, VA.)*

*Detail of the head of the preceding Mason swan.*

*Hunting pintails in California in 1923-note the Mason Detroit grade pintail rig.*

*Rare Mason swan - one of two birds mounted on entrance gate posts to a Back Bay gun club in Virginia. (Collection of the Refuge Waterfowl Museum in Chincoteague, Virginia.)*

*Mason's Decoy Factory ad with the cut showing a pair of Premier pintails - (Courtesy of The Sporting Goods Dealer.  July 1906.)*

142   SCHOVERLING, DALY & GALES

## WOOD AND TIN GAME DECOYS

### "Premier" Model Duck Decoys

Hollow and flat bottomed; the finest decoy ever made. The drawings for them were made from life, and as a consequence are mathematically correct, particular attention being paid to all fine details, such as shape of head, bill, arch of neck, etc. In hollowing them out, they are cut in two above the water-line, thus preventing any leakage. Being flat on the bottom, they ride the water exactly like the living bird and have not the rocking motion of the old-fashioned decoy in rough weather. The eyes used are the finest enamel, colored the same as the living birds. No pains have been spared to make these goods surpass anything in the shape of a decoy that has heretofore been manufactured.  Per dozen, . . . . . . . . . . . . $12.00

### "Challenge" Model Duck Decoys

With the exception of our "Premier," the best decoy made, and meets the wants of those who do not feel like paying what our "Premier" are worth, and yet desire a strictly fine decoy. These goods must not be confounded with the cheaper goods so common on the market. They are strictly what we represent them, viz.: the best that can be had at the price.

Per dozen, . . . . . . . . . . . $7.50

*Ad for Mason decoys from a 1912 Schoverling, Daly, & Gales Catalog.  Cut depicts the Premier blue wing and green wing teal and Challenge grade widgeon.*

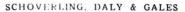

SCHOVERLING, DALY & GALES   143

## GAME DECOYS and DECOY CALLS

Robin Snipe    Golden Plover    Yellow Legs    Black Breast    Snipe

### Wood Snipe Decoys

Made from selected wood.  Painted, to represent perfectly, the different kinds of snipe.  A great many of these have been sold in the past, and greatly aid in hunting these birds.  We furnish varieties as shown in cut.

Per dozen . . . . . . . . . . . . . . . . . . . . . . . $3.50

*Ad from the same 1912 firearms catalog offering Mason wood snipe decoys for $3.50 per dozen.*

### Folding Tin Snipe Decoys

The best Snipe decoy ever put on the market. They are very light and when folded, pack into a very small space.  When set up, they are very lifelike in appearance, being carefully painted to resemble the live bird.  They come packed one dozen in a neat, black japanned tin case, as shown by cut.  Case has carrying handle and hasp lock, making a very serviceable carrying and storage case for the decoys.

All varieties . . . . . . . . Per dozen, $4.00
Extra supports, regular length . . Per dozen, .75
Extra supports, extra length . . . Per dozen, 1.50

### Crow Decoys

The finest Crow Decoy on the market.  Cut from solid wood block, well shaped and painted.  It is becoming popular to shoot crows over decoys, especially in closed season on other birds. . . . . . . . . . Per dozen, $5.00

*Ad from the 1912 Schoverling, Daly, & Gales Firearms Catalog with Mason crow decoys for sale, also tin snipe.*

*An old Remington U.M.C. ad from an October 1919 Field & Stream Magazine showing a waterfowl hunter with two of the finest models of duck hunting equipment a sportsman could outfit himself with in those days, a Remington Model 11 repeating shotgun and a rig of Mason Detroit grade goldeneye decoys.  The author uses an original Remington Model 11 for duck hunting today and could not ask for a better gun.*

*A fine original paint Detroit grade Mason bluebill. Mason must have sold many hundreds of bluebill decoys to gunners along the mid-Atlantic coast, because more Mason scaup turn up here than any other species. (Collection of the author.)*

130

Seven Mason decoy ads, all with the same cut of the Premier mallards, but different text. The advertising manager did not lack for imagination. The ads are dated from July 1910 to April 1924 and are from Outdoor Life Magazine, which was the earliest, Outing Magazine, All Outdoors Magazine, Field & Stream Magazine, and Hunter-Trader-Trapper Magazine, which was the latest. Curiously, there were six different street addresses.

An unusual pair of Mason 3rd grade glass eye canvasbacks in fine original paint - long slender pintail style bodies and heads very unlike canvasbacks, yet these birds are in original condition. (Collection of Dick McIntyre.)

131

*Challange grade broadbill, Mason Decoy Factory,
Detroit, Michigan, 1900. (Collection of the author.)*

*Hollow Premier grade scaup decoy by Mason
Decoy Factory, Detroit, Michigan, c-1905. (Collection of the author.)*

*Rare Mason Decoy Factory crow decoy. Apparently not many Mason crow decoys survived as few are found today and they are prized additions to any collection. (Collection of the author.)*

*Mason Decoy Company dowitcher in almost mint condition. (Courtesy Herbert Schiffer Antiques.)*

*Mason Detroit grade black duck - original paint.*
*(Courtesy Herbert Schiffer Antiques.)*

*Mason Decoy Company, Detroit Michigan Premier*
*scaup decoy. (Courtesy Herbert Schiffer Antiques.)*

**MINNESOTA RUBBER DUCK
COMPANY**

Spring Park, Minnesota

*Ad (Courtesy of Hunting and Fishing Magazine.*
*October 1941.)*

## NORTH AMERICAN DECOY COMPANY

Weston, Connecticut

The North American Decoy Company was the enterprise of well known sportsman, Ralf Coykendall, who wrote the excellent book *Duck Decoys and How to Rig Them*, and his son Ralf Coykendall, Jr. In operation in the late 1950's, the Coykendall's decoys were offered in a set of eight "natural" decoys with five drakes and three hens, all with different head positions or attitudes. These eight "natural" decoys were far more effective than several dozen, all in one position. They were made out of wood, combining hand work and machines, and finished with a realistic paint job.

The Coykendall's exclusive "reel keel" was fastened to the bottom of the decoy and made it much easier setting out or picking up the rig and reduced the amount of time that is usually required to untangle lines. A set of eight North American Decoy Company mallards sold for $56.00 in 1959. They were also offered in blackduck, pintail, canvasback, broadbill, redhead, and whistler.

*Pages from the 1959 North American Decoy Company catalog.*

# NORTH AMERICAN DECOY COMPANY
## WESTON                    CONNECTICUT

3 X

*We believe these are the finest decoys ever offered for sale*

NOTE "REEL KEEL." (See Page 13)

**DRAKE MALLARD FROM SET OF EIGHT**

6

**LEFT HEAD DRAKE**

**TURNED HEAD HEN SLEEPER**

**LOW HEAD DRAKE**

**LOW HEAD HEN**

**RIGHT HEAD DRAKE**

**HIGH HEAD HEN**

**HIGH HEAD DRAKE**

### SET OF 8 BROADBILL DECOYS

These Scaup decoys, five drakes and three hens illustrated above are used for Broadbill, Bluebill and Ring-neck ducks. They are oversize and are remarkably seaworthy. Even a few have great visibility.

**TURNED HEAD DRAKE SLEEPER**

10

**TURNED HEAD DRAKE SLEEPER**

**LOW HEAD HEN**

**LEFT HEAD DRAKE**

**HIGH HEAD HEN**

**HIGH HEAD DRAKE**

**TURNED HEAD HEN SLEEPER**

**LOW HEAD DRAKE**

### SET OF EIGHT MALLARD DECOYS

These fine, big decoys are outstanding. As illustrated the set consists of three hens and five drakes. The plumage painting has been perfected after years of testing. All who have shot over them consider them the world's finest.

**RIGHT HEAD DRAKE**

11

**HIGH HEAD BLACK DUCK**

**LOW HEAD BLACK DUCK**

**BLACK DUCK SLEEPER**

**CORK BLACK DUCK SLEEPER**

There are some gunners who believe that only cork makes a satisfactory Black Duck Decoy. For them we offer, at only a slightly higher price, a complete set of cork decoys.

**THE BLACK DUCK** is the most sagacious, wary and wildest of all the ducks and the most difficult to bring into range. The finest decoys are none too good. We make no effort to distinguish the sexes in plumage painting, but the set of eight does have the variety of head positions illustrated by the mallards on the preceding page. Dull finish paint is especially compounded for this decoy and we believe that they have no equal.

# OUTING MANUFACTURING CO.

## DEWEY'S METAL FOLDING DECOYS

Elkhart, Indiana

Patented in 1923, Outing Manufacturing Company which produced Dewey's Metal Folding Decoys does not appear to have advertised past 1925, although their decoys were produced much later than this date. The Dewey decoys were equipped with a patented spring leg which was adjustable according to the velocity of the wind. This imparted a life like motion to the decoy when the wind was blowing. They also made floating mallard decoys out of tin with a wooden bottom board. Their most popular offering seems to have been the "Crow Killer Combination" which included an owl decoy, two crow decoys, and a crow call for $7.50.

*Dewey's "Crow Killer Combination" with the original corrugated box - (Collection of Morton and Carol Kramer.)*

*Dewey's folding snipe decoy in original paint.
(Col lection of Dan Brown.)*

*Dewey's floating mallard decoy. (Collection
of Morton and Carol Kramer.)*

138

# PASCAGOULA DECOY COMPANY

Pascagoula, Mississippi

The Pascagoula Decoy Company was a separate and distinct decoy manufacturer that made decoys in Pascagoula that were very similar to those of the Animal Trap Company of Mississippi, which also operated in Pascagoula. The Pascagoula company made and sold their birds under the brand name or trademark of "PAD-CO." They were in business from at least 1941 to 1956 and in those fifteen years turned out thousands of Padco decoys that were sold by jobbers, hardware dealers, and sporting goods stores all over the country. Distinguishing their decoys from those of the conglomerate of companies that produced wooden birds for the Animal Trap Company is difficult at best. The model styles are somewhat variable and the paint patterns on the decoys of the two companies are distinctly different. The brochure reproduced here completely has much information on Padco decoys that I will not repeat in this writing. If one will take a stamped Animal Trap Company pintail, for instance, and compare it to the cut of Padco's pintail in the brochure the difference is easily discernible. One of the photographs included in this section displays the two different pairs of pintails side by side. Another clue is noted in the letter dated December 19, 1955 from Mr. L.C. Winterton, owner of Pascagoula Decoy Company to Mr. Joseph French, a long time collector of decoys. In it Mr. Winterton notes that the dowels on the Animal Trap Company heads are 5/8 inch in diameter while those used by Pascagoula are 1/2 inch in diameter.

How important the determination of who made which will be left to the discretion of the collector, but to the aficionado of "Pascagoula" decoys, this distinction becomes an important link in the study of the history and chronology of the Singing River Valley decoys.

*Ad (Courtesy of Outdoors Magazine. November 1941.)*

*Letter from Mr. L.C. Winterton, owner of Pascagoula Decoys to Mr. Joseph French. Several interesting notations are included in this letter which might help to point out the difference between Pascagoula decoys and those of Animal Trap.*

# PASCAGOULA DECOY COMPANY

Decoys
Paddles
Boat Oars
Saw Handles
Dimensions
Wood Turnings

— *Manufacturers and Distributors* —

SPORTING GOODS—WOOD SPECIALTIES
STAPLE WOOD PRODUCTS

P. O. Box 711 - Telephone 675

PASCAGOULA, MISSISSIPPI

November 26, 1955

Mr. Joseph B. French
Steelcote Manufacturing Co.
3418 Gratiot
St. Louis 3, Missouri

Dear Mr. French:

Your letter of the 17th and sample Decoy heads arrived last Monday
and we would have answered much sooner had we not been trying to get
some exactly like yours - which were made by Animal Trap Co. of America,
Lititz, Penn'a. However, they have discontinued making wooden heads,
even for their wooden Decoys, and are now using a hollow plastic head -
which looks pretty fragile.

We can supply you with wooden Mallard (or other species) heads from our
own patterns, with eyes installed and bored for dowels, unpainted, for
$5.00 per dozen, plus postage. But they are somewhat smaller and (we
think) look much better. Of which you can get some idea from the enclosed
catalogue folder. And we are returning your samples, along with one of
our's Monday - which will enable you better to decide if you want some.

(Incidentally, I notice your Decoys have 5/8" dowels. Ours use 1/2".
Otherwise we would include dowels at the same price. But we can bore
the heads to 5/8" if you want; and you can pick up some 5/8" dowel stock
locally - at Sears, or almost anywhere.)

If our pattern will serve your purpose on your present Decoys let us
know, and we will ship them within a few days - even though we don't try
to sell heads, since our head-lathe capacity can hardly keep up with our
own requirements. I just know that Decoys are very serious business to
those who use them - for I use them myself.

Now here is another suggestion: During the past almost 20 years it has
been our policy to sell to other manufacturers at our jobber prices, for
they, like us, sell mostly to jobbers - and we have never lost a jobber
because of that policy. So, whether you decide to fix up your old Decoys
or not, if we should receive an order from your Company it would be shipped
and billed them at the same prices at which we sell to people such as
Shapleigh Hardware Co. of your City, whom you no doubt know, and who, for
many years have been among our very best customers.

Possibly others in your organization, too, might want something in our
line - which might be pooled into a company order.

Sincerely,

L. C. Winterton, Owner

AIR MAIL

12/19/55

SHIPPED 1/3/56

VIA Parcel Post

**Invoice Nº 5540**

## Pascagoula Decoy Company
— *Manufacturers of* —
**W O O D   S P O R T I N G   G O O D S**
P. O. BOX 711
PASCAGOULA, MISSISSIPPI

DATE 1/3/56

SALESMAN

TERMS ok.with order

SOLD TO:

Joseph B French
Steeleote Mfg. Company
3418 Gratiot
St. Louis 3, Missouri

SHIPPED TO:

Same

| Quantity | Grade | Size | Article | Price | Amount |
|---|---|---|---|---|---|
| 1 Only | Standard | | Mallard DRAKE Decoy | | $1.00 |
| 1 Doz. | " | | "      Decoy HEADS, Unpainted but with eyes installed, bored for dowels but dowels NOT driven | | 4.00 |
| | | | | | $5.00 |

2548/ap

*Invoice from the Pascagoula Decoy Company.*

*Four page brochure of the Pascagoula Decoy Company, c-1955, (Courtesy of Joe French.) In the price list which accompanied this brochure Padco also listed the coot or poule-d'eau which gave them ten species offered for sale. They also manufactured and advertised for sale varnished or enamaled canoe paddles in spruce, cypress, oak, ash, maple, or cherry, ash boat oars, boat hooks and poles, saw handles, and wooden mitre boxes.*

# PADCO Duck DECOYS bring 'em in!

**ILLUSTRATED CATALOG**
All species, all grades, complete descriptions and prices.

**PASCAGOULA DECOY COMPANY**
PASCAGOULA, MISSISSIPPI

# PADCO *Duck* DECOYS *bring*

### Designed by Duck Hunters!

PADCO Duck DECOYS are designed by duck hunters, to look like live ducks — **to real ducks.** It's what **ducks** think of your decoys that counts. PADCO Duck DECOYS have been "duck-tested" for years with remarkable "pulling" results.

### Made of cork-like woods!

PADCO Duck DECOYS are made of kiln-dried Tupelo Gum and Pop Ash, the famous cork-like woods from the swamps of the "Singing River".

### Shaped by wood-carving craftsmen!

Each PADCO Duck DECOY is expertly shaped to real-life appearance and correct proportions to assure realistic "riding" on the water. The heads are carefully carved and permanently attached by means of a hardwood dowel and waterproof glue.

### Hand-painted by experts!

PADCO Duck DECOYS are impregnated with spar varnish for waterproofing, and then painted with the best grade flat paints especially manufactured for this purpose. Every decoy is hand painted to assure realism in color values and hues.

---

## MALLARD

HEN

DRAKE

**Body Size:** Approximately 5½" wide, 12½" long and 3¼" thick.

**Winter range:** The entire United States, southern and western Canada, and Mexico.

## PINTAIL

HEN

DRAKE

**Body Size:** Approximately 5½" wide, 12½" long (plus longer tail on Drakes) and 3¼" thick.

**Winter range:** Entire coastal areas of the United States, Mexico and Central America.

## RED HEAD

DRAKE HEN

**Body Size:** Approximately 5½" wide, 11" long and 3¼" thick.

**Winter range:** California, Mexico, and the Gulf Coast from Texas to Northwest Florida; and the Atlantic Coast from South Carolina to Massachusetts.

## RING-NECK

HEN

DRAKE

**Body Size:** Approximately 5½" wide, 11" long and 3¼" thick.

**Winter range:** Southeastern United States.

## SEE BACK PAGE FOR COMPLETE DETAILS

# ing 'em in!

### Preferred by experienced duck hunters!

PADCO Duck DECOYS have been "duck-tested" for years by experienced duck hunters in every section of the nation. Experienced hunters who have "tried 'em all" prefer PADCO Duck DECOYS because they have proven the remarkable "pull" of these "duck-tested" decoys.

### Built to last a lifetime!

PADCO Duck DECOYS are built to last a lifetime. They are made of solid cork-like wood, kiln-dried, impregnated with waterproofing Spar Varnish and painted with special high grade paint to assure years of satisfactory service.

### Economically priced!

PADCO Duck DECOYS are made in four grades as described on the back page of this folder. Each grade is a real value in its class and the range of prices make it easy for every sportsman to own genuine PADCO Duck DECOYS.

## BLACK DUCK

DRAKE AND HEN ALIKE

**Body Size:** Approximately 5½" wide, 12½" long and 3¼" thick.

**Winter range:** From the lower Rio Grand Valley northeast to Maine.

## BLUEBILL or SCAUP

HEN

DRAKE

**Body Size:** Approximately 5½" wide, 11" long and 3¼" thick.

**Winter range:** Entire coastal regions of the United States, Mexico and Central America, and the lower Mississippi valley.

## CANVASBACK

HEN

DRAKE

**Body Size:** Approximately 5½" wide, 11" long and 3¼" thick.

**Winter range:** Coastal areas of entire United States (except lower Florida) and Mexico.

## BALDPATE

HEN

DRAKE

**Body Size:** Approximately 5½" wide, 12½" long and 3¼" thick.

**Winter range:** Entire coastal areas of the United States, and Mexico.

## GOLDEN-EYE

HEN

DRAKE

**Body Size:** Approximately 5½" wide, 11" long and 3¼" thick.

**Winter range:** The Pacific slope, the Mississippi valley and Eastern United States.

TAILS, PRICES, PACKAGING INFORMATION

# PADCO *Duck* DECOYS

## available in four grades
## Packed ½ Drakes and ½ Hens

### "SUPREME"
#### GRADE

Our "Supreme" grade Decoys are made of the very finest and lightest Tupelo and Pop Ash obtainable. The bodies, heads and bills are hand finished and smoothly sanded; after which they are hand painted in natural colors and patterns, with special dull-finish paint. Truly a "Supreme" Decoy, exceptionally light in weight.

| Size Pkg. | Shipping Wt. | List Price |
|---|---|---|
| 1 Doz. | about 18 Lbs. | $30.00 |

### "STANDARD"
#### GRADE

Made of choice Tupelo and Pop Ash and shaped to the same patterns as our higher grades; with the same slightly-rough surface as the Top Flights and hand painted in natural colors, but with somewhat less detail; these decoys are a quality product at a very moderate price.

| Size Pkg. | Shipping Wt. | List Price |
|---|---|---|
| 1 Doz. | about 24 Lbs. | $19.00 |

### "TOP FLIGHT"
#### GRADE

Made of selected, lightweight Tupelo and Pop Ash, with surface finished slightly rough to produce that "feathered effect" preferred by many hunters, and hand painted in natural colors and patterns — to "pull the high flyers in." An extra quality, light-weight Decoy.

| Size Pkg. | Shipping Wt. | List Price |
|---|---|---|
| 1 Doz. | about 21 Lbs. | $24.00 |

### "SPECIAL"
#### GRADE

Made of Tupelo and Pop Ash but sometimes of heavier weight, this grade consists primarily of "seconds" culled out of the better grades because of overweight, slight blemishes and minor defects. Good, serviceable Decoys, made on the same body patterns as the high grades, our "Specials" are a real "buy" But orders are accepted only subject to available supply.

| Size Pkg. | Shipping Wt. | List Price |
|---|---|---|
| 1 Doz. | about 25 Lbs. | $15.00 |

Above list prices are subject to trade discounts to jobbers and dealers, who also may secure PADCO Duck DECOYS in assortments for sample or display purposes.

Orders from individuals who are unable to obtain PADCO Duck DECOYS from their dealers must be accompanied by full remittance and shipping charges will be C. O. D.

All prices are f. o. b. Pascagoula, Mississippi, and are subject to change without notice.

Write for FREE CATALOG of PADCO PADDLES AND OARS.

# PASCAGOULA DECOY COMPANY
## PASCAGOULA, MISSISSIPPI

Coot or poule-d'eau decoy by Pascagoula Decoy
Company. (Collection of Morton and Carol Kramer.)

Ad (Courtesy of Outdoor Life Magazine.
October 1942.)

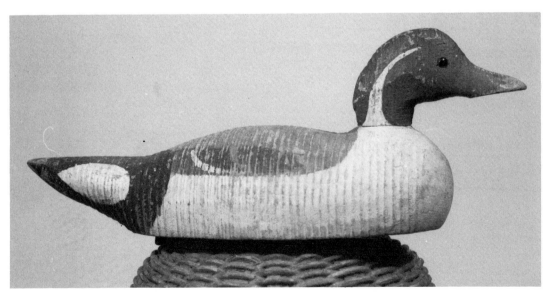

Pintail drake by Pascagoula Decoy Company-note
the almost identical appearance to the pintail drake
pictured in the Padco brochure. (Collection of
the author.)

Ad (Courtesy of Outdoor Life Magazine.
June 1943.)

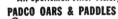

# PAW PAW BAIT COMPANY

Paw Paw, Michigan

The Paw Paw Bait Company of Paw Paw, Michigan, having taken over the Moonlight Bait Company, was one of the earliest makers of wooden fishing plugs in America. One of the early innovators, they produced many varieties of plugs that are very desirable to fishing tackle collectors today. In 1932 they decided to add wooden duck decoys to their line and for four years, through 1936, they manufactured six different species of ducks in decoys. They were made of Michigan pine or cedar and were offered in black duck, mallard, pintail, blue and green wing teal, and bluebill. They were hand painted and covered with a light flocking material to cut the glare. The bottoms of the decoys were stenciled with the name and address of the company.

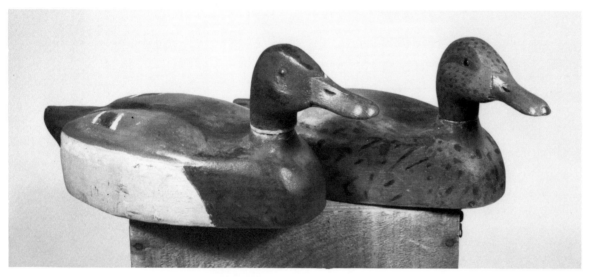

*An excellent original condition pair of Paw Paw mallards. (Collection of Morton and Carol Kramer.)*

*Bottom of the preceding mallards showing the stenciled Paw Paw name.*

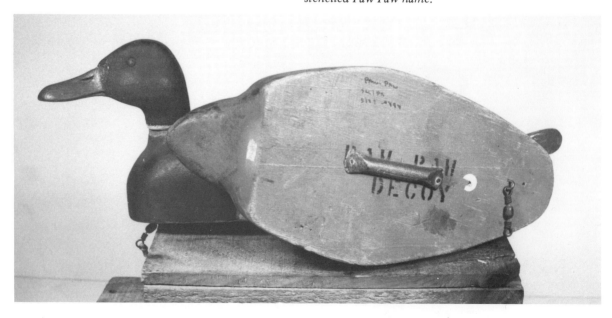

148

*High neck pintail drake by the Paw Paw Bait Company. (Collection of Tom Witte.)*

*Rare Paw Paw Company ringneck drake. (Collection of Tom Witte.)*

## GEORGE PETERSON

Detroit, Michigan

George Peterson was the predecessor to Jasper N. Dodge and he produced decoys of his own design from about 1873 to 1884, making him one of the earliest manufacturers of wooden duck decoys. The birds attributed to Peterson are very similar in many characteristics to some of the Mason decoys and few collectors feel certain of what distinctions constitute Mason from Peterson. The decoys that do lay claim to Peterson manufacture are beautiful decoys and a prized addition to any collection.

*Mallard drake attributed to George Peterson. Many collectors believe this style of decoy to be a Mason, while others claim it is Peterson. Whatever, it possesses handsome styling and paint. (Collection of Morton and Carol Kramer.)*

*A pair of mallards and an unusual painted black duck by Peterborough Decoy Factory located in Ontario, Canada. Attractively scratch painted and fitted with glass eyes, these decoys are the only factory examples to be found from Canada. (Collection of the author.)*

## PETERBOROUGH DECOY

## FACTORY

Peterborough, Ontario

These decoys appear to have been made only in the one grade pictured and are thought to have been done sometime during the 1920's. Mallards, black ducks, canvasbacks, redheads, and bluebills are known as of this writing, although other species may have been made that haven't been discovered by decoy collectors as yet. The earlier birds had fancy and elaborate paint styles while the later ones, such as those pictures, were scratch painted in a less fanciful design. They all were fitted with glass eyes. Most of the production was hollowed from the bottom with two- two inch bored holes. A small percentage are found hollowed in the manner of the Mason Premiers. The information on the Peterborough company is presented here through the courtesy of Hugh Valiant of Dauphin, Manitoba. The hen mallard in the photo was a gift from Mr. Valiant to the author.

*A hen mallard decoy by Peterborough Decoy Factory. (Collection of the author.)*

## POITEVIN BROTHERS, INCORPERATED

Pascagoula, Mississippi

The Poitevin Brothers decoy company's claim to familiarity lies in the knowledge that it was purchased in 1940 by the Animal Trap Company of America. Prior to that transaction, little information is known of the *"Singing River"* brand of decoys. Advertisements are reproduced here from 1927 and 1928 and a catalog was offered to prospective customers who would write in to the company. Perhaps one day, one of these catalogs will be discovered and a little more information on the earlier history of the Poitevin Brothers Decoy will come to light.

After the company and its facilities were bought by Animal Trap Company of America, the former Singing River brand decoys were manufactured under the brand name of Victor for the newly formed subsidiary, Animal Trap Company of Mississippi. It is doubtful that any distinction can ever be made between the Poitevin Brothers Decoy and the Victor Animal Trap decoy.

## WILLIAM E. PRATT MANUFACTURING COMPANY

Joliet and Chicago, Illinois

The William Pratt Manufacturing Company went into business in 1893 as a manufacturer of iron castings and hardware. Their production plant was located in Joliet, Illinois and the headquarters in Chicago. In 1920 the company began making wooden duck decoys as a seasonal sideline. With the purchase of the Mason Decoy Company equipment and materials in 1924, Pratt went full scale into the decoy business and produced birds year round. A former employee remembered once making one hundred and ten dozen decoys in one day. Thousands of Pratt decoys were sold all over the United States during the 1920's and 1930's by such companies as Von Lengengerke & Antoine, Abercrombie & Fitch and both Sears Roebuck and Montgomery Wards In a 1936 catalog Pratt offered nineteen different styles or models of decoys. When William E. Pratt died in 1939 the company was sold to Joslyn Manufacturing Company which in turn sold the decoy, mouse, and rat trap department to Animal Trap Company of America in Lititz, Pennsylvania.

*Ad (Courtesy of Outdoors America Magazine. November 1928.)*

*Ad (Courtesy of Hunting and Fishing Magazine. October 1927.)*

*Ad (Courtesy of Field & Stream Magazine. November 1928.)*

151

# Duck Decoys

We manufacture Duck Decoys of all species including the following varieties:

No. 1

Mallard
Canvasback
Red Head
Teal
Black Duck
  (Black Mallard)
Pintail (Sprig)

Blue Bill (Broad
  Bill)
Mud Hen (Am.
  Coot)
Widgeon
Scoter
Butterball
Whistler

Our Decoy Lumber is put through our own Dry Kiln to assure light weight and freedom from checking; the cedar blocks are then treated in a waterproofing solution and carefully painted several coats. The Decoys are of the proper shape, and all except Nos. 9, 17 and 18 have glass eyes. Heads are fitted on with dowels. Eight drakes and four hens are packed in a one-dozen crate. Except where noted decoys are painted with a dull finish to prevent glare. The letter F indicates rough or feather finish.

### Decoys are furnished regularly in the following styles:

| No. 1 or 1-F. | Solid. | Standard size, non-gloss finish. |
|---|---|---|
| No. 2 | Solid. | Mammoth size, long necks. |
| No. 2-A. | Solid. | Mammoth size, extra large with short necks. |
| No. 3 | Hollow. | Large size, smooth finish. |
| No. 4 or 4-F. | Airwood. | Large size, solid. |
| No. 5 | Solid. | Extra large, smooth finish, geese only. |
| No. 5-A. | Hollow. | Extra large, smooth finish, geese only. |
| No. 5-B. | Airwood. | Extra large, smooth finish, geese only. |
| No. 6 or 6-F. | Solid. | Flat pattern. |
| No. 8 or 8-F. | Airwood. | Flat pattern. |
| No. 9-F. | Solid. | Flat pattern, painted eyes. |
| No. 10-F | Solid. | Flat pattern, glass eyes. |
| No. 12-F. | Rival. | Standard size, feather finish, glass eyes. |
| No. 14 | Solid. | Hand carved. |
| No. 15-F. | Hollow. | Standard size, feather finish, glass eyes. |
| No. 16 | Ideal. | Hurd patent, wood base, steel body. |
| No. 17 | Profile | Wood. |
| No. 18 | Solid. | |
| No. 19 | Gazecki. | Self-contained anchors. |
| No. 20 | Solid. | Crows only. |
| No. 21 | Set-up. | Anchor, cord, and balance weight. |

No. 19—GAZECKI

No. 20—CROW

SPECIAL
DECOYS MADE
TO ORDER

No. 16—IDEAL

46

*Two pages from the 1936 Wm. E. Pratt Co. catalog showing the nineteen different models of decoys for sale.*

152

# Details of Decoys

**No. 1 and 6** Decoys are made from selected cedar, standard size, life-like heads and bodies carefully painted true to nature, glass eyes and are the highest grade of machine made decoys. All species.

**No. 2**—Decoys are 16½″ long instead of standard 14″ length and with long necks. Nicely finished and show up well in the water. All species

**No. 2-A**—Decoys are 17″ long, with short necks, for large bodies of water. where they have to be seen from a distance. Canvasbacks only.

**No. 3**—High Grade Hollow Decoys. Two pieces of wood hollowed out and joined with waterproof glue, same as formerly made by Mason, larger than the standard decoy.

**No. 4 and 8**—are made from airwood which is a South American Cane lighter than cork, does not crack, is strong, durable and takes paint well. These decoys, while expensive, are the very best decoys we make. All species.

**No. 5**—Decoys are Geese only; No. 5—solid; No. 5-A—hollow; the No. 5-B airwood.

**No. 9**—Decoys are standard size, flat pattern, with painted eyes.

**No. 10 and 12**—are feather finish, standard size decoys, water-proof paint. glass eyes, heads doweled on. They are made in Mallards, Bluebills, Canvasbacks and Pintails.

**No. 14**—Decoy is high-grade, hand carved, beautifully finished and painted, long thin neck, graceful body, selected stock, the very best decoy obtainable. Includes balance weight, anchor and cord, all ready for use.

**No. 15**—Decoy is the standard size cedar decoy, same as No. 12 except that it has cylindrical space hollowed out to reduce the weight.

**No. 16**—Hurd Decoys have a pressed steel body, detachable wooden head and base, are quickly assembled, pack into less than a cubic foot of space, are very light and durable; make a most life-like appearance on the water. Size 2½″ thick, 13½″ long.

**No. 17**—are Profile Decoys made in any species, of inch material. Imitation glass eyes, 10″ high and 15″ long; take little room; can be staked on the ground, or floated in the water in sets of three or five, on a platform. Decoys are furnished without stakes or platforms:—these are supplied on special orders.

**No. 18**—are solid decoys made in Mallard, Bluebill, Canvasback and Pintails. Have imitation glass eyes, heads fastened to body with piece of steel, machine finished with ordinary paint; from log run lumber. A cheaply made and finished decoy.

**No. 19**—The Gazecki Decoy has a device similar in operation to a window shade inserted in a 2 inch hole bored into the bottom of the decoy The anchor is fastened to the cord wound on a spool. When setting out decoys the desired length of cord is withdrawn. Taking in the decoys a simple pressing of a lever causes the springs to wind up the cord. No balance weights are necessary with this decoy. The device can be furnished separately for inserting in decoys or any of our decoys can be equipped with this. Price is for the device alone. When decoys are equipped ready for use the cost is the total of the cost of device. plus cost of installation in the decoy, plus cost of the decoy.

**No. 20**—is a Crow Decoy only. It is solid, the size of a crow, with jet black finish, glass eyes, wire stakes to use in fastening to trees, fence posts, or placing on the ground.

**No. 21**—is the equipment required for every decoy. No. 4 Balance Weight, screws for attaching, 8 ft. cotton cord, No. 1-A anchor; packed in individual carton. Can be sold to every decoy purchaser.

*Pratt Company goldeneye drake in the feather finish. (Collection of Dan Brown.)*

*Pratt Company crow. (Collection of Ron Gard.)*

*An old Pratt pintail, c-1920's that has seen a lot of hard gunning and yet still retains the ability to do the job for which it was originally intended. (Collection of the author.)*

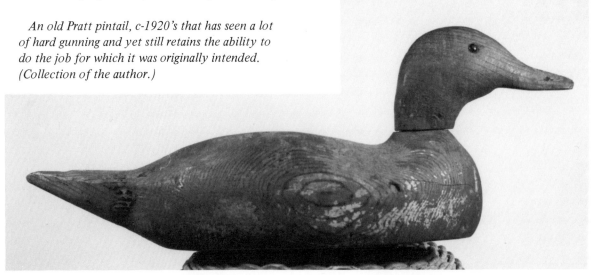

*Wm. E. Pratt Company canvasback - smooth finish and hollow with fancy paint. (Collection of Les Brown.)*

*A Mississippi Flyway goose hunter with a snow goose by the Wm. E. Pratt Company, c-1940.*

The hunter sees a duck passing at 80 yards, lets off both barrels at once, and makes a kill

*An Illinois duck hunter with Pratt Company decoys, c-1934.*

*A Wm. E. Pratt Company dipper. (Collection of the author.)*

*A Wm. E. Pratt Company rare white wing scoter decoy with the feather finish. (Collection of the author.)*

*Ad (Courtesy of Outdoor Life Magazine. April 1925.) The cut bears a striking resemblence to a Mason Premier mallard.*

*Two smooth finish Pratt drake goldeneyes in
excellent original paint. (Collection of the author.)*

An outstanding hollow, smooth finish Pratt drake
bluebill in mint unused condition. This is their top
of the line model - note the fancy paint patterns.
(Collection of the author.)

Original paint Pratt Company goose decoy. (Collection of Morton and Carol Kramer.)

## OSCAR QUAM COMPANY

Spicer, Minnesota

Oscar Quam began making cork decoys for sale to hunters in 1928 and his catalog in the 1960's showed a full and complete line of decoys and associated water-fowling equipment. Though very simple in design and paint, they more than adequately do the job for which they were intended. Information and photo of mallard decoys courtesy of Dick Lancaster.

*Ad (Courtesy of Sports Afield Magazine. 1937.)*

*Ad (Courtesy of Outdoor Life Magazine. October 1945.)*

*Oscar Quam cork mallard drake - the ballast lead with the raised letter Quam name can be seen on the bottom of the hen mallard.*

## REALISTIC DECOY COMPANY

Kewaunee, Wisconsin

These decoys were made by Alois Luker under the trade name of Realistic Decoy Company in Kewaunee. They were made during the years 1932 - 1939 and are known in canvasback, bluebills, and mallards. They resemble the Evans style of decoy made also in Wisconsin.

*A pair of Realistic Decoy Company canvasbacks in original paint. (Collection of Roger Ludwig.)*

# J.W. REYNOLDS DECOY FACTORY

Chicago, Illinois

Established in 1904, James Reynolds made three different styles of decoys during the period his business was in operation. He probably produced hand made V-board decoys from 1904 until about 1909 when he applied for a patent on his second identifiable style of decoy, the "Automatic Canvas Decoy Ducks." These were very similar to the Acme Folding Canvas Decoys and consisted of a printed canvas covering over a collapsible wire frame that was attached to a wooden bottom board. When not in use, they folded nearly flat for ease in carrying and storage. A wire stem pushed forward from the rear of the duck raised the framework and the decoy became fully formed. The late Mr. Willis Pennington, a noted midwestern decoy collector, recalled hunting over a rig of J.W. Reynold's canvas decoys when he was a boy. He relates that they performed ably unless a strong wind or rough water interuppted and then the light weight decoys had trouble. The bottom boards were stenciled with the name and address of the factory.

Reynolds also made full bodied wooden decoys which were called Reynolds "Lucky" wooden decoys. Mr. Pennington felt that these birds were turned out on the Wm. E. Pratt Company duplicating lathes and then painted and sold by Mr. Reynolds. They are very similar in style to the Pratt or Animal Trap Company's "feather or rough finish" decoys and it could well be true that he farmed out the

*A pintail drake by J.W. Reynolds that is identical to No. 22 in the 1973 Session IV of the William Mackey collection. (Courtesy of Ron Gard.)*

actual turning of the decoys. James Reynolds was a true artist though, and little doubt is left as to who may have made these factory decoys with the circular blade marks if they are finished with an elaborate showy paint pattern applied.

The last type of decoy that will be mentioned that was produced by the J.W. Reynolds Company was the Illinois River wooden folding decoy ducks. These may have been the first type that he developed and were V-boards made with three silhouette decoys attached to a spring loaded floating frame. They folded into a light, compact, easy to carry decoy and a half dozen could be handled almost effortlessly. When rigged out on the water they would represent eighteen individual duck decoys. These V-boards were also painted in an elaborate, sophisticated fashion.

Mr. Reynolds also advertised wing flapping crow, owl, and duck decoys and although these have not been identified by the collector, it is certain that they would prove to be interesting and colorful additions to a decoy collection.

Most of this information on the Reynolds Factory was obtained from the Willis Pennington article in the 1977 *Decoy Collector's Guide* through the courtesy of its editor, Mr. Harold Sorenson of Burlington, Iowa.

A folding Illinois River decoy V-board by J.W.
Reynolds. (Collection of Dan Brown.)

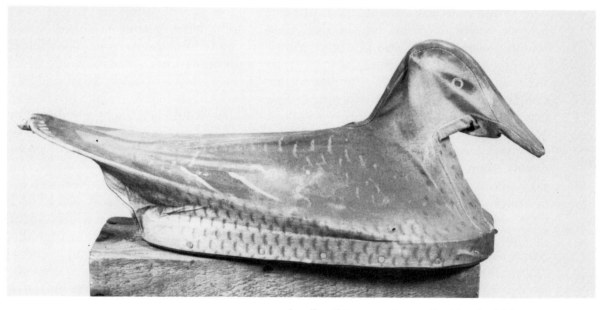

The bottom board of a collapsible canvas decoy
showing the J.W. Reynolds Company stencil and
the wire stem at the rear that is pushed forward
to erect the framework.

A collapsible canvas hen mallard by the J.W.
Reynolds decoy factory in nice original condition.
(Collection of Morton and Carol Kramer.)

*Folding canvas mallard drake by J.W. Reynolds Company in excellent original condition. (Collection of Les Brown.)*

# Decoys

*Ad (Courtesy of Fur-Fish-Game Magazine. October 1937.)*

*Cuts used for the early ads placed in newspapers and magazines by J.W. Reynolds Company. (Collection of Dick Lancaster.)*

*Ad in the 1906 Sporting Goods Dealer.*

# REX DECOY COMPANY

Los Angeles, California

# RILEY DECOY CORPORATION

Eugene, Oregon

A plastic decoy whose head dips down into the water when a line is pulled. Raised letters on the keel read RILEY MECHANICAL DECOY, RILEY DECOY COR., EUGENE, OREGON.

*Ad (Courtesy of Outdoor Life Magazine. November 1934.)*

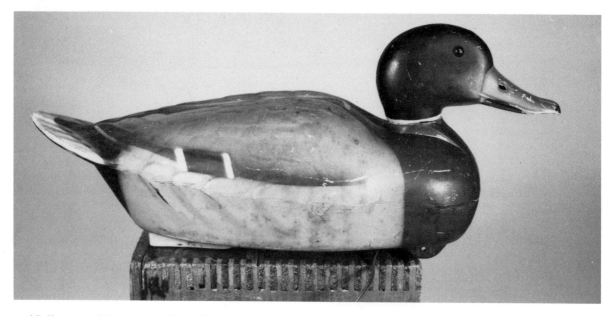

*(Collection of Morton and Carol Kramer.)*

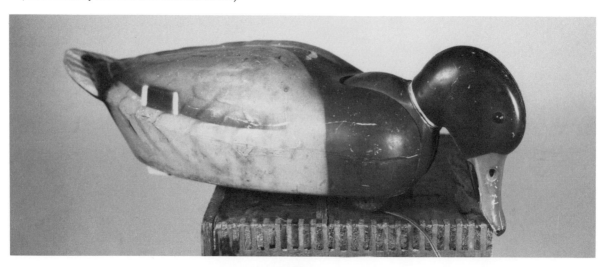

# THE ROSE FOLDING DECOY

Chicago, Illinois

The Rose Folding Decoy was an early all wooden folding decoy that had a one inch thick bottom board and a thinner silhouette that sprung upright and snapped into place. They were lightweight, small, and had fine colorful paint pattern.

SPECIAL SALE
$9.50 DOZEN

2 Dozen
limit to
an order.

50 Dozen for September sale. Never again sold at this price. Regular price $12. Send money with order or no sale price guaranteed. ROSE FOLDING DECOY, 4432 N. Campbell Ave., Chicago

*Ad (Courtesy of Outdoor Life Magazine. September 1926.)*

### Duck Hunters Asking Us This Season for Rose Folding Decoys

Sure proof they are O. K. Glass eyes. Perfect color, live action. Have you tried them? $12.00 prepaid per dozen. They fold up small and fool them all.

**THE ROSE FOLDING DECOY**

4432 N. Campbell Ave.    Dept. C.    Chicago, Ill.

*Ad (Courtesy of Outdoor Life Magazine. October 1921.)*

Rose Folding Decoy

"It folds up small. and fools 'em all"

Floats, acts and looks like a live duck. It's light and always ready. The only wooden folding decoy showing full body on the market. *If your dealer won't supply you—write.* Price $11 doz. The Rose Folding Decoy, 4432 N. Campbell Ave., Dept. F, Chicago

*Ad (Courtesy of Outdoor Life Magazine. October 1923.)*

*A Rose folding hen bluebill decoy in original paint. (Collection of Dan Brown.)*

165

## W.J. RUPPEL COMPANY

Sheboygan, Wisconsin

What little is known about the Ruppel decoys points to the cork birds as their most popular offering. They also apparently made decoys in balsa and cedar in most all species. They were in production from about 1938-1944.

Cork Decoys

**HAND MADE FOR ALL SPECIES**
**Life-like and durable**
*Write for circular*
W. J. RUPPEL CO., Sheboygan, Wisc.

*Ad (Courtesy of Field & Stream Magazine. August 1939.)*

# Nation's Finest Hand Made
## duck and geese decoys

CORK

Balsa, cork, cedar. $12. per dozen and up. If your dealer can't supply you, write direct, including your dealers name. No postcards acknowledged.
**W. J. Ruppel Co., Sheboygan, Wisconsin, P.O. Box 477**

*Ad (Courtesy of Outdoor Life Magazine. October 1940.)*

*Cork hen mallard decoy by W.J. Ruppel Company. (Collection of Roger Ludwig.)*

*Bottom of the hen mallard showing the stenciled name and location of the company.*

## SEARS ROEBUCK AND COMPANY

Sears Roebuck and Company sold many thousands of decoys made by most of the major decoy companies from J.N. Dodge to Victor Animal Trap. Decoys have been offered through their catalog since before 1900 and continue to be offered today. Sometime after World War II Sears had manufactured for them their own J.C. Higgins brand of composition fibre or paper mache decoys similar in construction and style to the paper mache Animal Trap, Ariduck, and Carry-Lite products; they had their own markings on the bottom. Initially a paper label with the name J.C. Higgins was affixed and later the name was impressed into the bottom by raised letters on the mold.

*J.C. Higgins molded paper mache decoy, a black duck. (Collection of the author.)*

*J.C. Higgins paper mache hen canvasback, c-1946 and hen mallard, c-1956 in all original condition. (Collection of the author.)*

## SOULES AND SWISHER

Decatur, Illinois

This company either produced or distributed molded fiber composition or paper mache crow shooters kits consisting of a two faced owl and two crows. The facts are not clear and the S&S owl and crows have been included in a General Fibre Company advertisement leading to the theory that

General Fibre or Ariduk produced the birds for Soules and Swisher. Ariduck had its own paper mache crow shooters kit and the owl was completely different from the S&S bird while the crows were identical which helps confuse the issue even more.

*Soules and Swisher two faced owl. (Collection of Morton and Carol Kramer.)*

*Ad (Courtesy of Outdoor Life Magazine. November 1948.)*

NEW THRILLS... MORE SHOOTIN'

DID You "BAG" Your Limit Last Year?...No?

THEN Hunt Crows —Season Always Open—No Limit!

## CROW SHOOTERS' KIT

Here are the crow decoys you need to bring in the flock...Kit contains 1 sensational S & S TWO-FACED OWL and 2 AIRCROWS...Users get results...Nationally Famous...Nationally Advertised. Dept. O

$5^{00}$ SET

AT YOUR DEALER OR ORDER DIRECT (Add 2% Sales Tax if located in Mo.)

The HUNTERS CO. 1722 ST. CHARLES ST. LOUIS 3, MO.

168

## PAUL A. SPERRY DECOYS

New Haven, Connecticut

If the decoys made by Paul Sperry really look as good as those in the advertisement, then someone somewhere should have a rig of, perhaps, or maybe just one, good looking collectible decoy. It would be very interesting indeed to be able to find and identify a few of these attractive appearing decoys by these obscure makers for whom we have nothing more than a cut in an advertisement to tempt us. It is interesting to note that the balsa decoys cost double what the cedar birds cost in 1923.

*Ad (Courtesy of Field & Stream Magazine.
September 1923.)*

## H.A. STEVENS DECOYS

Weedsport, New York

Harvey Stevens was born in 1847 and died in 1894. Sometime around 1880 he began advertising decoys for sale in national sporting journals. His birds were all handmade and for that reason his production was considerably less than most of the other manufacturers of wooden decoy ducks. The earlier Stevens birds have been referred to as the humpback style and they are flat bottomed. Later he changed the style to an almost oval shaped, rounded bottom decoy. The lines of this style are truly classic and combined with the outstanding paint patterns make for a beautiful piece of work. Most of the Stevens decoys have an inletted staple for attachment of the anchor line and one to three flush lead ballast weights melted into one inch bored holes. Harvey Stevens stenciled his name and address on the bottom of most of his decoys. However, there are fine original condition decoys known that are unquestionably Stevens that lack the stenciled identification. One round bottom bird in the collection of Dr. Morton Kramer of Baltimore has the name "G.W. STEVENS, WEEDSPORT, N.Y." branded in the bottom. Possibly this was Harvey Stevens' brother George. Some of the finest Stevens decoys extant reside in the collections of George Thompson of Cazenovia, New York and Dr. Peter Muller of Atlanta, Georgia.

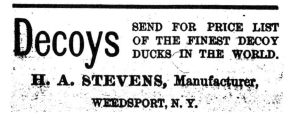

*A Stevens advertisement for decoys in the August 28, 1884 issue of Forest and Stream Magazine.*

Stevens "humpback" model bluebill in original
paint. (Collection of Morton and Carol Kramer.)

Exceptional Stevens black duck decoy, rounded
bottom model. (Collection of Bill Butler.)

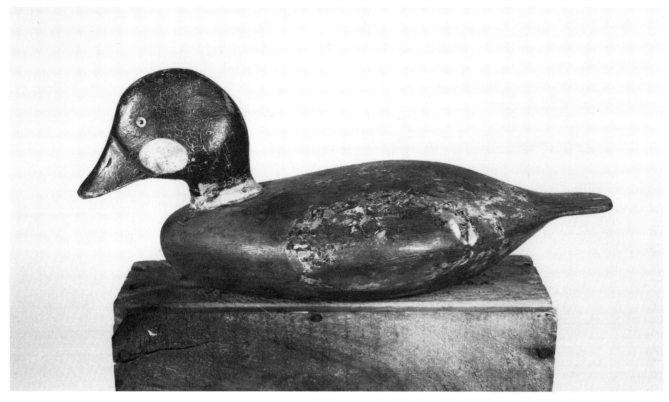

*Stevens goldeneye drake with the unusual brand in the bottom. (Collection of Morton and Carol Kramer.)*

*Stevens decoy with the brand "G.W. STEVENS, WEEDSPORT, N.Y." in the bottom. (Collection of Morton and Carol Kramer.)*

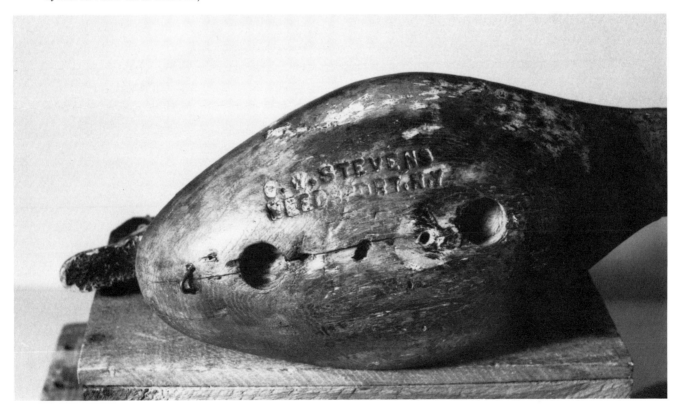

## STRATER AND SOHIER
Boston, Massachusetts

These two men revolutionized the design of the shorebird decoy at the early date of 1874 by developing the initial idea of the hinged folding decoy. Made of stamped embossed tin and hand painted in extremely realistic feather patterns, they were a boon to the snipe hunter. Nestled together when opened, the gunner could carry a dozen of these birds as easily as three or four of the bulkier wooden stool. They came packed one dozen to a tin box and included wooden stakes with a piece of copper tubing split to hold the molded leg piece on the bird. This stake with the two top wire hinges held the bird together when in use and allowed it to be set up in the mud or sand when rigged for hunting.

Most of these early "tinnies" had the name and patent date stenciled inside. Some had "S & S" and the patent date, some "Strater & Sohier" and the patent date, and others just the patent date of "Oct. 27 '74." When Herman Strater and William Sohiers patent rights ended, thousands of tin folding birds were produced by a number of eastern companies. Most of these birds are very collectible, but may remain forever unidentified.

Strater and Sohier also included hollow stamped tin ducks in their production and a fine original condition black duck is pictured in Mr. Mackey's *American Bird Decoys* on page 236, Plate 186.

*Strater and Sohier folding tin sanderling. (Collection of the author.)*

*A folding tin snipe rig set out at Great Kills, Sta-
ten Island in the 1920's - four ruddy turnstones
and a semipalmated sandpiper are in the background.*

*Ruddy turnstone "tinnie" in original condition
made by Strater and Sohier. (Collection of the author.)*

*Original tin box of one dozen yellowlegs and their stakes as manufactured by Strater and Sohier before 1900. (Collection of Morton and Carol Kramer.)*

*Strater and Sohier yellowleg, dowitcher, and plover tin decoys. All of these birds have the patent date stenciled inside. (Collection of the author.)*

*A very unusual and rare tin folding plover probably intended as a semipalmated plover. (Collection of Ted Harmon.)*

*Three folding tin snipe by Strater and Sohier of Boston, Massachusetts. The small tin "peeps" are particularly hard to find in original condition. (Collection of Dan Brown.)*

175

## TECHRITE CORPORATION

San Gabriel, California

## W.D. TRIMBLE

Baltimore, Maryland

An advertisement was located for "W.D. Trimble, Wooden Ducks, 838 W. Lexington St. Baltimore" in the second annual edition of the Sportsmans Directory and Yearbook by Pond and Goldey of Milwaukee, Wisconsin in 1891. As far as is known, no decoys have been identified as having been made by W.D. Trimble.

*Ad (Courtesy of Field & Stream Magazine.)*

## TRU-DUX

Chicago, Illinois

Al Ries began making decoys for his own use in the early 1930's because he was displeased with the results of the commercial blocks that he was then using for duck hunting. After trials in cedar and cork Al began making mallard decoys out of balsa and offered them for sale commercially in about 1939. The demand for his well carved and excellently painted decoys was almost overwhelming and Al was overloaded trying to keep ahead of orders for his ducks that first year. He offered and sold twelve decoys in a compact carrying case that allowed the hunter to easily carry the lightweight birds to his favorite hunting ground. Later Tru-Dux made some pintail and bluebill decoys and one special order of wood ducks. There is a pair of the wood ducks on display at the Shelburne Museum in Shelburne, Vermont and they are a fine addition to the prestigious Shelburne collection. Al Ries and his brother Earle stopped making Tru-Dux in 1949, storing all equipment, patterns, and models. A fire shortly afterward destroyed everything.

# W. D. TRIMBLE.
## DECOY DUCK.

No. 378,410.                    Patented Feb. 21, 1888.

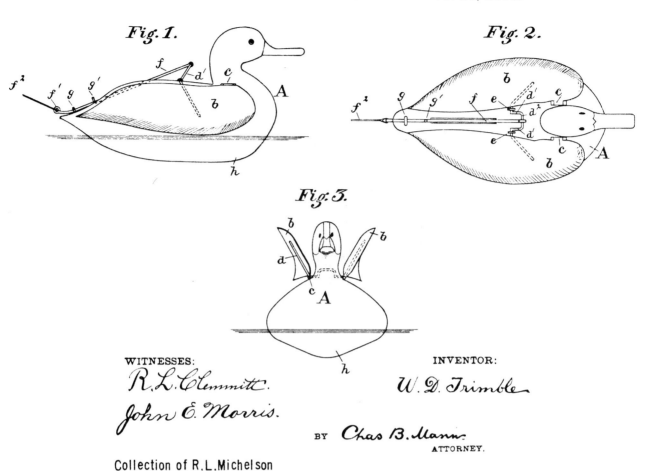

WITNESSES:

*R. L. Clemmitt.*

*John E. Morris.*

INVENTOR:

*W. D. Trimble*

BY *Chas B. Mann*
ATTORNEY.

Collection of R.L.Michelson

*Patent drawing for W.D. Trimble Decoys patented in 1888 illustrating that he designed a wing flapping decoy. Whether or not any of these decoys have ever turned up is not known. Apparently some were made as Trimble was advertising them for sale in 1891. Drawing (Courtesy of Toller Trader - originally published by Murray Mitterhoff of Springfield, New Jersey.)*

*A pair of "Tru-Dux" balsa mallards in original condition by Al Ries of Chicago, Illinois. (Collection of Morton and Carol Kramer.)*

## TUF-SKIN DECOY COMPANY

Minneapolis, Minnesota

Another canvas covered stuffed decoy that might be able to be identified by the cuts in the advertisements.

*Ad (Courtesy of Field & Stream Magazine. October 1939.)*

*Ad (Courtesy of Hunting and Fishing Magazine. November 1939.)*

## TUVESON MANUFACTURING

## COMPANY

St. James, Minnesota

Little concrete information on the Tuveson Company and the history of its decoy making operation is known, but their grotesque "flyers" seemed to have captured the fancy of a number of modern decoy collectors. One of these flying black ducks is pictured in the book *Chesapeake Bay Decoys* edited by Bob Richardson and published in 1973. It is pictured on page 107 with a cork "quacking" decoy and a K-D Company mallard. The picture is captioned "Gadgetry" and a better title for this photo would be hard to imagine. It seems that either Tuveson or Harry

V. SHOURDS OF Tuckerton, New Jersey received the inspiration for their flying decoys from the other for the canvas constructed wings over a wire frame are just about identical. There the similarity comes to a screeching halt.

Tuveson also produced cork decoys as early as 1928 and a good cut of one of their cork bluebills shows in one of the advertisements. They also offered cedars but whether this referred to their flyers, which appear to be made of cedar, or floaters that they might have made, it is not known.

*Flying Tuveson black duck with canvas wings and cedar body. (Collection of Morton and Carol Kramer.)*

**CORK Decoys**

The lightest, most life-like and durable decoy made. The decoy all old time hunters are demanding. At your dealers or direct.
**Tuveson Manufacturing Co., St. James, Minn.**

*1928 advertisement showing Tuveson cork decoy. Ad (Courtesy of Field & Stream Magazine. November 1928.)*

**DECOYS** CORKS
CEDARS
*Free Catalog*
Tuveson Mfg. Co., St. James, Minn. FLYERS

*Ad (Courtesy of Field & Stream Magazine. October 1934.)*

*Ad displaying the Tuveson "flyers" in the October 1930 Outdoor Life Magazine. (Courtesy of Decoy Collectors Guide, Burlington, Iowa.)*

**OLD TIME DECOY AD** OCT. 1930 OUTDOOR LIFE

**LOOK!!!**
**Flying Decoys**

PATENTED

AGAIN, Tuveson leads the field with a line of flying decoys in addition to the regular cork and cedar floating decoys. If there's ducks flying, you'll get them with this line-up. Here's a decoy that brings them in to you. Flying ducks always gather. That's why Tuveson's Flyers are so effective—the ducks see the Flyers and join the party.

If you want the best shooting you've ever seen, you'll find out about these Flyers. Made in every species—all natural as life set on rods and supported by a submerged wooden float, set up and taken down in a jiffy—and easy to carry. Hunters who have used them say there's nothing like them—especially if ducks are scarce. Write for full details and prices.

**TUVESON MFG. COMPANY**
721 4th Ave., No.
ST. JAMES, MINNESOTA

**Submitted by Harvey P. Richardson, Jr.**

179

# TUX-DUX

Madison, Connecticut

Another cork decoy offered in the late 30's and early 40's that resembles in style several other models from that period. Distinguishing one product from another and identifying the maker will probably take more luck than good honest research even though this company appears to have been in business for close to ten years.

### • CORK DECOYS
*—for the man who wants the best*
**SOLID OVERSIZE CARVED MODELS**
Sample—$2.25 prepaid in U. S. A.
*Write for Circular*
**TUXIS WOOD PRODUCTS CO., MADISON, CONN.**

*Ad (Courtesy of Field & Stream Magazine. November 1940.)*

**CORK DECOYS**
**For the Man Who Wants the Best**
**T U X - D U X**
Box 494                    Madison, Conn.

*Ad (Courtesy of Outdoor Life Magazine. October 1946.)*

*Ad (Courtesy of Field & Stream Magazine. November 1928.)*

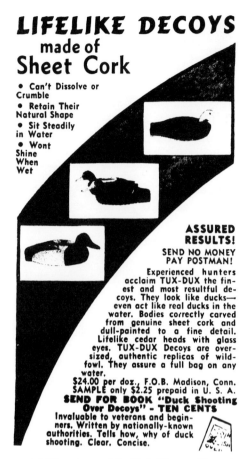

## LIFELIKE DECOYS
### made of Sheet Cork

• Can't Dissolve or Crumble
• Retain Their Natural Shape
• Sit Steadily in Water
• Wont Shine When Wet

**ASSURED RESULTS!**
SEND NO MONEY
PAY POSTMAN!

Experienced hunters acclaim TUX-DUX the finest and most resultful decoys. They look like ducks—even act like real ducks in the water. Bodies correctly carved from genuine sheet cork and dull-painted to a fine detail. Lifelike cedar heads with glass eyes. TUX-DUX Decoys are over-sized, authentic replicas of wild-fowl. They assure a full bag on any water.
$24.00 per doz., F.O.B. Madison, Conn.
SAMPLE only $2.25 prepaid in U. S. A.
**SEND FOR BOOK "Duck Shooting Over Decoys" - TEN CENTS**
Invaluable to veterans and beginners. Written by nationally-known authorities. Tells how, why of duck shooting. Clear. Concise.

*Ad (Courtesy of Field & Stream Magazine. October 1939.)*

*Ad (Courtesy of Field & Stream Magazine. August 1923.)*

## WOOD DECOYS
World's Standard Wood Decoys, all sizes, kinds and species. Also balance weights, anchors, live decoy halters. Catalogue free.
**VAN FLEET MFG. CO., JOLIET, ILL.**

## Decoy Ducks
We can make immediate shipment of first-class solid wood decoys with glass eyes. All species at $10.00 per dozen.

**VAN FLEET MFG. CO.**
**JOLIET, ILL.**

## VAN FLEET MANUFACTURING COMPANY

Joliet, Illinois

This company and Makutchan Roller B. Company of Joliet, Illinois must have been one and the same company, because they had identical ads in two different magazines in November 1928. The Makutchan Roller B. Company ad was in Hunting and Fishing Magazine and the Van Fleet Manufacturing Company ad in Field & Stream Magazine, both issues dated November 1928. If their decoys looked the same as the cut in their ads, they must have been hard to distinguish from Mason Premiers.

## MAKUTCHAN R.B. COMPANY

Joliet, Illinois

The two advertisements reprinted here are the extent of the information that the author was able to obtain on the Makutchan cedar decoys.

## L.T. WARD & BRO.

Crisfield, Maryland

The decoy making of Lem and Steve Ward of Crisfield Maryland very nearly took a turn toward commercialization in the mid 1950's. An entrepreneur decided that maybe the Ward Brothers gunning model decoy could be molded out of styrofoam and he persuaded Lem to carve wooden patterns for use in making the mold. This Lem did and apparently a mold was made which produced the two models shown in the accompanying photograph. The original wooden carved head is shown and it has the date 1954 and Lem's signature on the bottom. Informed sources reveal that after seeing the models Lem and Steve became disenchanted with the whole scheme and the project was dropped. Looking back today, it appears that the brothers, in their astute foresight, made a wise decision to halt an endeavor that might possibly have diminished the integrity of their great carvings.

*Ad (Courtesy of Field & Stream Magazine. November 1934.)*

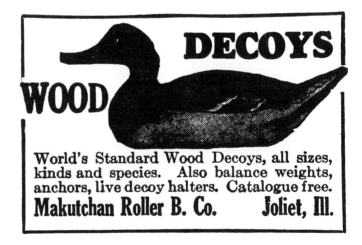

*Ad (Courtesy of Hunting and Fishing Magazine. November 1928.)*

*Ad (Courtesy of Field & Stream Magazine. October 1930.)*

*Two styrofoam models of 1955 era Ward Brothers hunting decoys. Original wooden carved head to the right. (Collection of Morton and Carol Kramer.)*

## WATERLOO DECOY COMPANY

Waterloo, Iowa

*Ad (Courtesy of Outdoor Life Magazine. August 1940.)*

*No further information on M.C. Wedd or his decoys has been uncovered since Bill Mackey mentioned them and pictured one of the decoys attributed to Wedd in his book* American Bird Decoys *published in 1965. The advertisement for decoy ducks for $5.00 per dozen that is reproduced here appeared in the August 28, 1884 issue of Forest and Stream Magazine.*

## M.C. WEDD

Rochester, New York

No further information on M.C. Wedd or his decoys has been uncovered since Bill Mackey mentioned them and pictured one of the decoys attributed to Wedd in his book *American Bird Decoys* published in 1965. The advertisement for decoy ducks for $5.00 per dozen that is reproduced here appeared in the August 28, 1884 issue of Forest and Stream Magazine.

## C.V. WELLS

Milwaukee, Wisconsin

C.V. Wells decoys were made of canvas covered cork bodies with wooden heads. They were manufactured from 1936 to 1944 and were made in mallards, canvasback, bluebills, coots, blue wing teal, and Canada goose. Wells also made flying decoys with wings out in tin covered with canvas. They were supported over water or field by a steel rod. Photos and information courtesy of Roger Ludwig.

*C.V. Wells cork black duck with a canvas covering and wooden head. (Collection of Roger Ludwig.)*

*Bottom of Wells black duck showing stencil of name and address.*

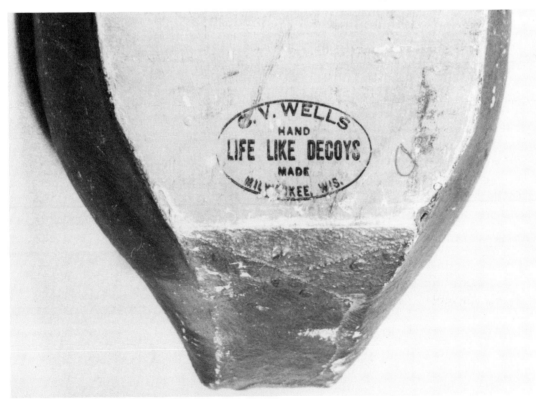

# WILDFOWLER DECOYS

Old Saybrook, Connecticut

Edward H. "Ted" Mulliken founded the Wildfowler Decoy Company in 1939 and produced some of the finest wooden working decoys out of white pine and balsa that ever came off of duplicating lathes. Ted had made and painted excellent hunting decoys for his own use for a number of years before deciding to go into business manufacturing wooden decoys for other waterfowl hunters. Some of his early hand made work is in the collection at the Shelburne Museum at Shelburne, Vermont. A particularly fine hen bufflehead and ruddy duck are on display there. Within three years after Wildfowler went into production, the United States entered World War II and Ted soon turned his production into gun stocks under a contract with the government. After the war he switched his decoy material from white pine to government surplus balsa and the bulk of the Wildfowler decoys were made of this wood, with special orders being made of pine or cedar. All of the heads were made of white birch. The birds were offered in almost all species and quite a number of different models. They were available in a No.1 or No.2 finish; No.1 being an elaborate hand painted design with feathering, and No. 2, a simpler spray painted pattern listed as the gunners model. Ted, with several employees, continued to make gunning stocks at Old Saybrook until 1958 when he sold the company and Wildfowler name to Robert H. Standiford of Long Island. Mr. Standiford moved the equipment to his shop at Quogue, on the South Shore of Long Island and made decoys out of balsa that were very similar to those made at Old Saybrook. The birds made at Quogue had heads that were slimmer and exhibited less carving around the bills and faces. Also, many of the Old Saybrook birds were made with heads and necks inletted slightly into the body. All of the Quogue decoys appear to have been made with the necks resting on top of the body. At both locations some of the decoys were branded with the

Wildfowler brand and some weren't. In 1961 the business was sold to Charles Birdsall of Point Pleasant, New Jersey and he continued to make the quality Wildfowler decoys at his location along the New Jersey coast until the mid-70's. The company was then purchased by Amel and Karen Massa of Babylon, New York and they are producing the decoys there to the present day. The interesting aspect of collecting Wildfowler decoys is that each location of the company had their own brand with the company logo and location on it and many of the decoys at each location were branded and thus documented for future collectors. Again, it should be mentioned that not all Wildfowler decoys were so branded.

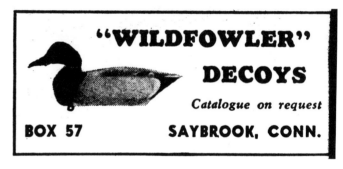

*Ad (Courtesy of Field & Stream Magazine. October 1939.)*

*Ad (Courtesy of Field & Stream Magazine. November 1943.)*

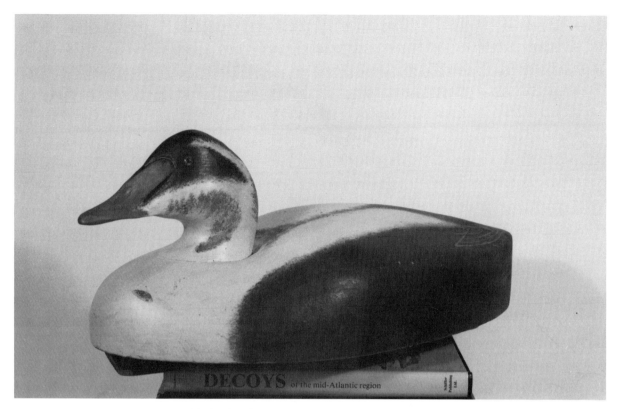

*Rare common eider decoy by Wildfowler, Old
Saybrook, Connecticut. Oversize Atlantic Coast
model. (Collection of Bill Butler.)*

*Coot decoy in the Atlantic Coast model, Wild-
fowler, Old Saybrook, Connecticut. (Collection
of Dan Brown.)*

*Hen pintail decoy - the headless feeder model by Wildfowler, Old Saybrook, Connecticut. (Collection of Dan Brown.)*

*Drake bluebill decoy, the Atlantic Coast cork model by Wildfowler, Old Saybrook, Connecticut. (Collection of Dan Brown.)*

*Hen mallard decoy, Atlantic Coast model by Wildfowler, Old Saybrook, Connecticut. (Collection of the author.)*

*Hen goldeneye decoy, Superior model by Wildfowler, Old Saybrook, Connecticut. (Collection of the author.)*

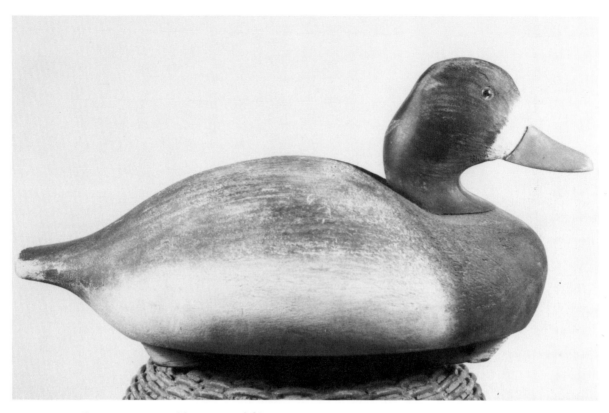

Hen bluebill decoy - oversized battery model in
No. 2 finish by Wildfowler, Old Saybrook, Connecticut. (Collection of the author.)

Black duck tip-up feeder decoy by Wildfowler,
Old Saybrook, Connecticut. (Collection of the
author.)

*Wildfowler Decoy Company canada goose made
at the old Saybrook, Connecticut shop. (Courtesy
of Herbert Schiffer Antiques.)*

*Wildfowler decoys*
*Top, from left - Old Saybrook tucked head black duck, a rare pair of Quogue blue wing teal hunting decoys as last rigged.*
*Middle - A pair of Superior Model Old Saybrook goldeneye.*

*Bottom - An outstanding pair of turned head sleeper pintails made at Old Saybrook, Connecticut.*
*All of the above (collection of R.H. Richardson.)*

190

*A lovely Superior model Old Saybrook drake green wing teal - very rare. (Collection of Ron Gard.)*

*A rare sleeping or preening hen bluebill made by Chuck Watson at Quogue Wildfowler Company when he was working for them in the late 1950's. (Collection of the author.)*

# WILDFOWL

## WINNERS 1941 THROUGH 1951

IN THE MACHINE MADE DECOY DIVISION, WILD
RIBBON, INCLUDING, "BEST MACHINE MADE D

Mallard Drake (Medium Neck)

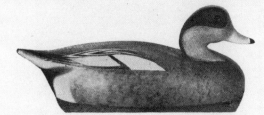

Pintail Drake (High Neck)

Widgeon Drake

Red Head Drake

Bluebill Drake

Whistler Drake

Pintail Hen (Medium Neck)

Widgeon Hen

## NEW SUPERIO
(Illust

Our new Superior Model retains the distinctive
features of the old model, namely, one-piece
head and neck, keel, different head positions, etc.
We believe it is the finest decoy ever offered.
Although the same length as the old model, approximately 14", depending on species, it is now made
wider (about 7") and with a longer bottom which
insures lifelike buoyancy in both rough or calm
water. It is made in selected heavy density Balsa, at
the above price. In Hollow Pine to order, only. The
weight of either material is approximately the same.
All joints are cemented with waterproof airplane glue
and the finest glass eyes are used. They are hand
painted in detail and are highly recommended particu-

Canada Goose

# R DECOYS

OWLER DECOYS HAVE WON EVERY IST and 2ND
COY IN SHOW," AGAINST ALL COMPETITION.

Black Duck Drake (High Neck)

Canvasback Drake

## MODEL No. I

(ted)

larly in the marsh duck species where a lifelike decoy
is essential to good shooting. Made regularly in
Mallard, Pintail, Black Duck, Widgeon (Baldpate), Blue
and Greenwing Teal, Canvasback, Red Head, Bluebill
or Whistler (Goldeneye). Any species to order at slight
extra charge. Packed eight drakes and four hens unless
otherwise specified. Head positions per doz., Mallard
and Black Duck (Shipped 12 medium heads per doz.,
unless otherwise ordered. 3 straight head sleepers and
3 high necks may be included to the doz. at no extra
charge). Pintail—6 high, 6 medium. Other species—
6 medium, 6 low.

10% extra for special assortment.

### GOOSE DECOYS

Approx. size 20" x 9½" x 5"

Body made from best quality insulating Cork
with 1" bottom board or in heavy density balsa.

**Brant — 16" x 8" x 5"** (Not illustrated)

All models with keels.

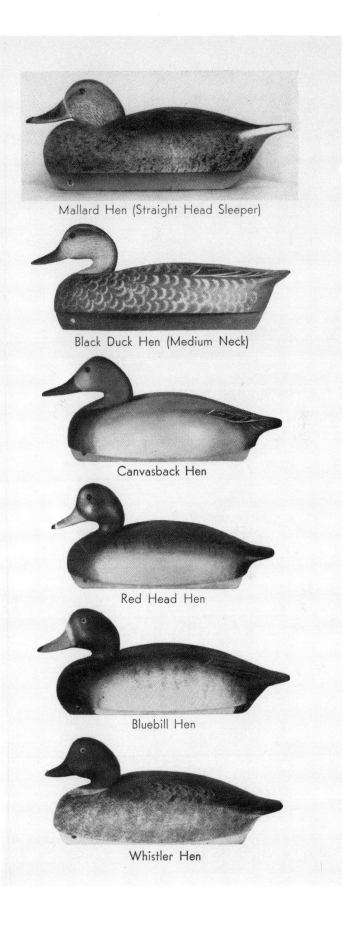

Mallard Hen (Straight Head Sleeper)

Black Duck Hen (Medium Neck)

Canvasback Hen

Red Head Hen

Bluebill Hen

Whistler Hen

Mallard

**BLACK DUCK** — Size approx. 17½" x 8½" x 4½"
Made in Black Duck and Mallard in Heavy Density Balsa or Cork.

Broadbill

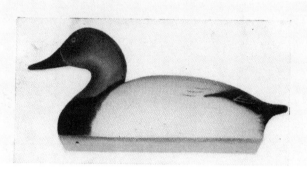

**CANVASBACK** — Size approx. 14½" x 8½" x 4"
Made in Canvasback, Red Head and Broadbill in Heavy Density Balsa or Hollow Pine to order.

Hand-made Oversize decoys have been in use for many years in some sections of the country, particularly in Maine and Mass. They have become increasingly popular and have a distinct advantage in being visible to the ducks at a much greater distance.

Black Duck

Made in Heavy Density Cork or Balsa, with or without keel. With keel unless otherwise specified.

The Atlantic Coast Model was first introduced in 1941 but was discontinued after the war, except on special order. We have had repeated requests from our customers to stock this model and are now able to comply. These decoys are approximately the same size as our Superior Model but are more rugged and the painting follows the pattern as used by professional guides without the complete detail of our Superior Model. They are recommended for hard usage and where a large rig of decoys is used.

**COOT**

Made to order in Balsa, Pine or Cedar.

## DECOY HEADS

Complete with dowel and glass eyes.

Painted Unpainted

## DECOY KITS — Retail only

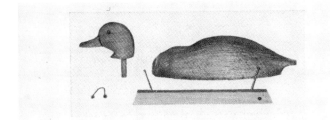

Made in Balsa only in Superior or Atlantic Coast Model kit consisting of body, head, eyes, dowels and keels. Heads and bodies drilled but not sanded, ready for assembly.

These knocked-down decoy kits are made of best quality materials for the duck hunter who has his own idea of painting and detail.

Black Duck, Mallard, Pintail, Widgeon, Canvas-back, Redhead, Bluebill, Golden Eye.

## DECOY LINE

Heavy tarred line that will stand hard usage. Comes in 300 foot coils.

## ANY DECOY MADE TO ORDER

# WILDOWLER DECOYS
## (INCORPORATED)

## OLD SAYBROOK
## CONNECTICUT
## 1953-1954

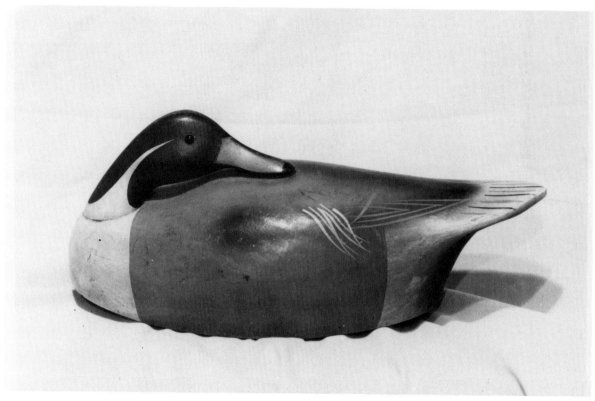

*An outstanding drake pintail turned head sleeper made by Wildfowler, Quogue, New York. (Collection of Herbert Schiffer Antiques.)*

*American crow decoy by Wildfowler Decoy Company, Point Pleasant, New Jersay. (Collection of Art Birdsall.)*

*"Seagull" decoy made by Wildfowler Decoy Company, Point Pleasant, New Jersey. (Collection of the author.)*

197

# Unknowns, Gadgetry & Live Decoys

In this short section will be included a number of photographs of factory decoys by unknown makers. Dozens of photos of decoys of apparent commercial manufacture whose origin was unfamiliar to anyone who had seen them were scrutinized and some of the more interesting or those that had distinct characteristics in their carving, painting, or style were selected for inclusion here. Also contained in this chapter are a few advertisements for unusual contrivances to do with decoys or duck hunting and several ads for decoys that did not really deserve a place in the alphabetical order in the main section of the book. Finally this section will encompass some rather intriguing ads for paraphenalia associated with live decoys or "tollers,"

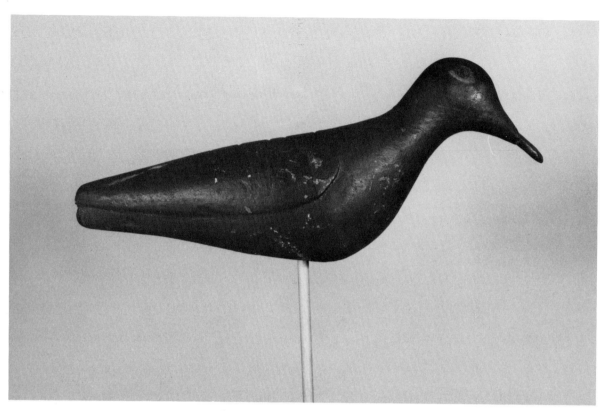

*Unknown snipe made of wood, iron tack eyes, has "J.H. Co." on bottom. Formerly in the Mackey collection, now owned by Morton and Carol Kramer.*

*Unusual oversize hen mallard with the brand "L.FISHER" and a bird on the bottom, glass eyes. (Collection of Morton and Carol Kramer.)*

*Cork brant decoy with a spindle carved head of pine. (Collection of Dan Brown.)*

*A very nice unknown mallard drake decoy, hollow carved with a bottom board, very pleasing original paint, painted eyes. (Collection of Dan Brown.)*

Unknown tip-up feeder decoy, painted as a mallard drake, a long iron rod with a lead weight on one end that swings freely from the front end of the decoy - could possibly be made by the Rex Decoy Company of Los Angeles, California. (Collection of Morton and Carol Kramer.)

An attractive pair of mallards in original paint, similar to a number of different makers in carving style, but the paint is altogether different. (Collection of Morton and Carol Kramer.)

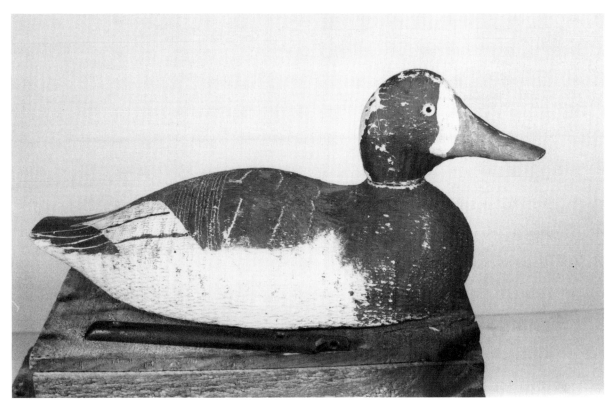

Unknown bluebill hen in fine original paint, glass
eyes. (Collection of Morton and Carol Kramer.)

Duck Flash Decoys - $6.00 a dozen in 1940 means
something is funny here. Ad (Courtesy of Outdoor
Life Magazine. October 1940.)

Material was somewhat less expensive forty years
ago. Ad (Courtesy of Sports Afield Magazine.
March 1940.)

Ad (Courtesy of Outdoor Life Magazine.
October 1940.)

*Ad (Courtesy of Outdoor Life Magazine. October 1946.)*

*This may be an advertisement for J.M. Hays decoys that was in the 1923 catalog of Charles Williams Store.*

*Ad in the 1894 - 95 Montgomery Wards Catalog-may be Acme Folding Canvas Decoys.*

*The Novelty Sales Company of Memphis, Tennessee offered for sale several different styles of decoys that they called Eureka Decoys - several of their ads are shown here. Sports Afield 1943-44; Hunting and Fishing Magazine. October 1938; Field & Stream. October 1941.*

*A rare folding tin tern decoy by an unknown manufacturer - the only one known of its kind, this bird is similar in construction to the tin snipe decoys also owned by Ted Harmon. (Collection of Ted Harmon.)*

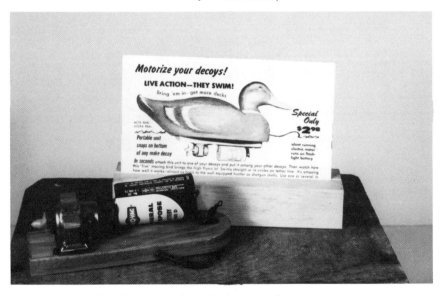

*A motorized device to attach to the bottom of any decoy. (Collection of Morton and Carol Kramer.)*

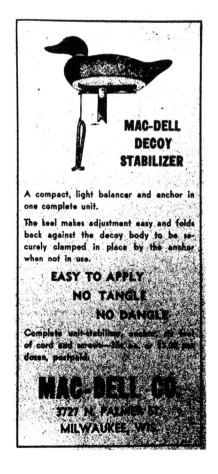

*The Mac-Dell Decoy Stabilizer - Ad (Courtesy of Sports Afield Magazine. 1943-44.)*

*Unknown folding tin plover by one of the numerous factories that followed Strater and Sohier, made after 1900. (Collection of the author.)*

*Unknown composition mallards. These birds are molded hollow out of some kind of a cork like composition with wooden movable heads. (Collection of the author.)*

206

Unknown black duck in original scratch paint. Sure to be identified after appearing in print, this bird's maker is unknown at the time of this writing. (Collection of the author.)

*The Pitts Adapter - ad (Courtesy of Outdoor Life Magazine. September 1926.)*

*Another pair of molded cork composition mallards by an unknown maker, in original condition. (Collection of the author.)*

*A black duck decoy in original paint said to be copied by a New England factory after a Crowell bird. The maker is unknown at this time. (Collection of the author.)*

*A mammoth oversize canvasback by an unknown maker as compared to a standard size Dodge canvasback in the foreground. The mammoth decoy may have been made on a special order by the William E. Pratt Company. (Collection of the author.)*

*A canvas covered shorebird decoy by an unknown maker. A lot of these decoys have shown up on Nantucket Island and are often referred to as "Nantucket rag bags." They have wooden bills and nice paint work. (Collection of the author.)*

*Oversized factory ruddy duck found in North Carolina. A wooden machine turned body with a stamped tin head, in original paint. (Collection of the author.)*

*Unknown canvasback decoy in original paint.
Another bird that should be identified as soon
as other collectors see it. The carved bill work and
swirled breast scallop paint are prominent characteristics. (Collection of the author.)*

*Hen canvasback factory decoy by an unknown maker. This entire bird is made of a molded composition type material and has a wooden bottom board. It is spray painted and has glass eyes. (Collection of the author.)*

*Two hen canvasbacks by an unknown maker.
Original paint with nice feathering and glass eyes.
These birds for years have turned up in the Chesapeake Bay area with such regularity that most collectors from this region are sure that they were
made close by. They may have been special ordered
from some factory out of the area in the Chesapeake Bay style body though, because the paint
style is not typical of this locality. Any further
information on these birds would be appreciated
by the author. (Collection of the author.)*

*Miniature paper mache mallard decoy made as
a salesman's sample or decorative item. (Collection
of Dan Brown.)*

*Unknown paper mache owl decoy - possibly made
by Molded Carry-Lite of Milwaukee, Wisconsin.
(Collection of Morton and Carol Kramer.)*

*Canvas covered Canada geese in mint original condition of unknown manufacture. Believed to have been made in the west, they were found on the Eastern Shore of Maryland which draws goose hunters from all over the world to its famous shores and cornfields. (Collection of the author.)*

*Canada goose decoy - molded paper mache body with a cellulose plastic removable head. Maker unknown. (Collection of the author.)*

*Hunters in the midwest setting out a rig of the preceding canvas covered goose decoys.*

*Unknown canvas covered cork goldeneye, similar in style to the Herter's decoy of this type, all original condition. (Collection of Ron Gard.)*

*Canvas covered canvasback decoy with inserted wooden bill - stenciled Scott Decoy Company on bottom - c-1900-1915. (Collection of the author.)*

*Unknown molded pigeon decoy. (Collection of Dan Brown.)*

216

## LIVE DECOYS

Until 1935 when their use was outlawed, many waterfowl hunters in North America supplemented their decoy rigs with a few live "tollers," "ducks or geese specifically trained for the purpose of decoying into gun range their wild brethren. There were duck farms that raised these decoys from the egg and supplied hunters all over the country, but many guides and local gunners raised and trained their own birds. In many instances a favorite "toller" was treated almost as well as the retriever who fetched the downed birds to his master. There is a photo in the July 1973 issue of the old *Toller Trader,* published by Murray Mitterhof of Springfield, New Jersey that shows Chris Sprague with one of his favorite "caller" geese named "Billie Burke." The story goes that the goose used to follow Chris around town as a puppy dog would a child. In Harry Walsh's book, *The Outlaw Gunner,* an engaging story is told of a live goose "caller" named "Old Pete." Whether this tale was a product of Dr. Harry's fine storytelling imagination or based on real facts, it points out how intelligent a bird the Canada goose could be when trained and employed as a live "toller." When the quality of duck and goose shooting began to deteriorate in the 1930's, the hunter received part of the blame, particularly the meat hunter.

Conservationists, sportsmen, and naturalists had been searching for a good argument for their side in the fight to ban live decoys and baiting and the drastic decline in the favorite sport of many of them was a cause strong enough to warrant action in this direction. In 1935 baiting to bring waterfowl into gun range and the use of live decoys was declared illegal and passed into law. Another era in the history of wildfowling had come to an end.

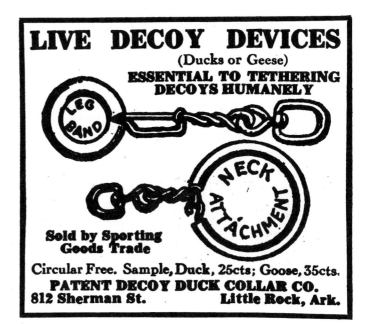
*Classified ads in the October 1923 issue of Out-
door Life advertising live decoys and callers for
sale.*

*Advertisement for decoy callers for sale by Tom
Reed of Chincoteague, Virginia, in the October
1923 issue of Outdoor Life Magazine.*

*Ad for live decoys from Oshkosh, Wisconsin.
(Courtesy of Outdoor Life Magazine, November
1931.)*

*English call ducks were more reliable than our
local mallards - classified offering the English birds
in Outdoor Life Magazine, November 1931.*

*Live decoy devices. Collars and leg bands for
live decoys. Ad (Courtesy of Hunting and Fishing Magazine. November 1928.)*

*Decoy harness. Ad (Courtesy of Outdoor Life
Magazine. October 1934.)*

*W.A. Gibbs & Son live duck decoy anchor attachment - Chester, Pennsylvania. Ad (Courtesy of Outdoor Life Magazine. October 1923.)*

*The Merrymeeting Bay Duck Strap. Ad (Courtesy of Field & Stream Magazine. August 1923.)*

*Duck callers from Missouri. Ad (Courtesy of Field & Stream Magazine, November 1935.)*

*Live decoys from the famous Wallace Evans Game Farm in Illinois. Ad (Courtesy of Field & Stream Magazine. December 1923.)*

*Ad (Courtesy of Field & Stream Magazine. November 1934.)*

*Ad (Courtesy of Field & Stream Magazine, November 1934.)*

*Live mallard decoys. Ad (Courtesy of Field & Stream Magazine, December 1923.)*

# GOOSE HUNT

GET YOUR LIMIT ANY DAY! Businessmen, lawyers, doctors, anyone can use this new, easy, quick sportsmanlike method. No crawling, just walk up, take pictures, then shoot. No pits, no decoys, no fraud. Send $25, name, address; I'll send you my secret. Guaranteed to work! Benton Coleman, Bridgeport, Wash.

A pen of live trained Canada geese decoys. These birds are penned right in front of the blind. 1934.

A black duck shooter on the Eastern Shore of Virginia returning with his game and cages of live decoys. 1935.

The Fly Ag'in Decoy Harness. Ad (Courtesy of National Sportsman, November 1938.)

Did anyone ever send for this man's secret?

After live decoys were banned from use in 1935, the ingenious waterfowl hunter naturally turned to mounted duck and goose decoys. Witness this Iowa goose shooter in 1939. A rig of decoys such as these are popularly used on the Eastern Shore of Maryland today.

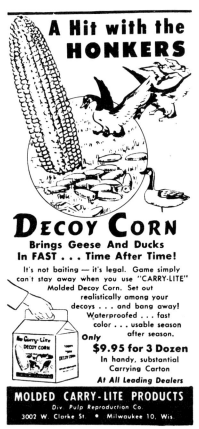
*Paper mache corn by Molded Carry-Lite Co. Milwaukee, Wisconsin. Ad (Courtesy of Field & Stream Magazine. October 1954).*

*Ad (Courtesy of Sports Afield Magazine. August 1950).*

*Ad (Courtesy of Field and Stream Magazine. October 1956).*

*Ad (Courtesy of Outdoor Life Magazine. November 1951).*

*Ad (Courtesy of Field and Stream Magazine. October 1958).*

*Ad (Courtesy of Field & Stream Magazine. October 1948).*

*The Minnesota duck chair. Ad (Courtesy of Sports Afield. October 1946).*

*Ad (Courtesy Sports Afield Magazine. July 1946).*

## "Spelling Their Finish"

*A rig of cork and wooden factory decoys. The wooden birds on the right appear to be Pratt or Animal Trap Co. Decoys.*

Retrieving fowl as quickly as you can after they are shot will eliminate much loss.

# RETRIEVING

*A duck hunter retrieves his game from among his rig of lathe turned factory decoys. Thousands of these wooden decoys were commonly used throughout the mid-west in the 1940's.*

*Duck hunters setting out their rig of factory decoys in 1948 on Rice Lake, Illinois.*

Below is a short list of the names of individuals or companies that sold decoys commercially-nothing more than a name and location are known.

1. Adams Decoy Company-Hickman, Kentucky

2. Ashert Brothers-Los Angeles, California

3. Bucklure Company-Newark, Missouri

4. Burkhard's Decoys-St. Paul, Minnesota

5. Cape May Company-Cape May, New Jersey

6. Classic Woodcarving-New York, New York

7. Dans Duck Factory-Quincy, Illinois

8. C.A. Frakes-Port Arthur, Texas

9. Gladwin Decoy Works-Frederic, Michigan

10. Grubbs Manufacturing Company-Pascagoula, Mississippi

11. J.P. Hendricks Company-Santa Barbara, California

12. W.H. Megarry Company-Worcester, Massachusetts

13. Modern Decoy Company-New Haven, Connecticut

14. Natural Duck Company-Topeka, Kansas

15. E.A. Nelson-Ludlington, Michigan

16. Wm. Read & Sons-Boston, Massachusetts

17. Real-Lite Decoy Company-Kansas City, Missouri

18. David C. Sanford Company-Bridgeport, Connecticut

19. Tryon Company-Philadelphia, Pennsylvania

# "Right in the blind, By Gosh!

"I TELL you, Bill, they don't fly half a mile after you hit 'em with Infallible."

**HERCULES**
*Smokeless Shotgun Powders*
**INFALLIBLE** and **E.C.**

**HERCULES POWDER CO.**

902 King Street

Wilmington       Delaware

*Our booklet "A Talk About Hercules Sporting Powders" will be sent at your request.*

# Bibliography

*American Bird Decoys*- William Mackey, Schiffer Publishing, 1980.

*The Art of the Decoy* - Adele Earnest, Clarkson Potter, 1965.

*Chesapeake Bay Decoys* - R.H. Richardson, editor, Crow Haven Publishers, 1973.

*Decoy Collectors Guide* - Hal Sorenson, editor, 312 Franklin Street, Burlington, Iowa, 1963-77.

*Decoy World Magazine*- M. Clark Reed, Jr., editor, 1978.

*Decoy Magazine* - Jeff Williams, editor, Aberdeen, Maryland.

*Decoys of the Atlantic Flyway* - George Starr, Jr., Winchester Press, 1974.

*Decoys of the Mid-Atlantic Region* - Henry Fleckenstein, Jr., Schiffer Publishing, 1980.

*Factory Decoys* - John and Shirley Delph, Schiffer Publishing, 1981.

*Shorebird Decoys* - Henry Fleckenstein, Jr., Schiffer Publishing, 1981.

*Toller Trader Magazine* - Murray Mitterhoff, Springfield, New Jersey, 1971-73.

*Wildfowl Decoys* - Joel Barber, Windward House, 1934.

# Suggested Reading

BOOKS SUGGESTED FOR FURTHER READING ON DECOYS

Barber, Joel- *Wild Fowl Decoys*-Originally published by Windward House in 1934, available now from Dover Publications - in print.

Berkey, Barry - *Pioneer Decoy Carvers* - 1977, Tidewater Publishers - available now - in print.

Buckwalter, Harold R. - *Susquehanna River Decoys* - 1978, Harold Buckwalter - available now - in print.

Cheever, Byron - *Mason Decoys* - 1974, Hillcrest Publications. Available now in print.

Cheever, Byron, editor - *North American Decoys* - Quarterly Periodical. No longer being published - some back issues available.

Colio, Quintina - *American Decoys* - 1972, Science Press. Available now - in print.

Delph, John and Shirley - *Factory Decoys,* 1981, Schiffer Publishing. Available now - in print.

Ernest, Adele - *The Art of the Decoy* - originally published in 1965 by Clarkson N. Potter. Available now in reprint. Will be back in print spring 1982, Schiffer Publishing.

Fleckenstein, Henry Jr. - *"Decoys of the Mid Atlantic Region"* - Schiffer Publishing, 1979.

Fleckenstein, Henry Jr. - *"Shorebird Decoys"* - Schiffer Publishing, 1980.

Frank, Charles W. - *Louisiana Duck Decoys* - 1975, Charles W. Frank. Available now - in print.

Giacoletta, Bernie and Rae - *The Decoy Hunter Magazine,* 1981, Clinton, Indiana. Available now - in print.

Johnsgard, Paul A., editor - *The Bird Decoy* - 1976, University of Nebraska Press. Available now - in print.

Kangas, Gene and Linda - *National Directory of Decoy Collectors* 1978-81. Available now - in print.

Mackey, William - *American Bird Decoys* - originally published by Dutton in 1965, available now from Schiffer Publishing Limited 1979 - in print.

McKinney, Evans - *Decoys of the Susquehanna Flats* - 1978, Holly Press. Available now - in print.

Mitterhoff, Murray - *Toller Trader,* Springfield, New Jersey, 1971-73. No longer being published, some issues still available.

Murphy, Stanley - *Martha's Vineyard Decoys* - 1978, David R. Godine. Available now in print.

Parmalee and Loomis - *Decoys and Decoy Carvers of Illinois* - 1969, Northern Illinois University Press. Original hardbound edition out of print, available now in softcover.

Reed, M.Clarke, editor - *Decoy World* - Quarterly periodical - no longer being published, some back issues available.

Richardson, R.H., editor - *Chesapeake Bay Decoys* - 1973, Crow Haven Publishers. Available on the rare book market - out of print.

Sorenson, Harold D. - *Decoy Collectors Guide* -1963-1979. Harold D. Sorenson, Burlington, Iowa. Available now - in print.

Starr, George, Ross, Jr. - *Decoys of the Atlantic Flyway* - 1974, Winchester Press. Available now - in print.

Townsend, Jane - *Gunners Paradise* -Wildfowling and Decoys on Long Island - Museums at Stony Brook, 1979. Available now - in print.

Walsh, Harry - *The Outlaw Gunner* - 1971, Tidewater Publishers. Available now - in print.

Walsh, Roy - *Gunning the Chesapeake* - 1961, Tidewater Publishers. Available now - in print.

Webster and Kehoe, David and William - *Decoys at Shelburne Museum* originally 1961, Shelburne Museum. Available now 1971, Shelburne Museum - in print.

Williams, Jeff - *Decoy Magazine* - Aberdeen Maryland 1979-81. Available now - in print.

# Index

## A

## B

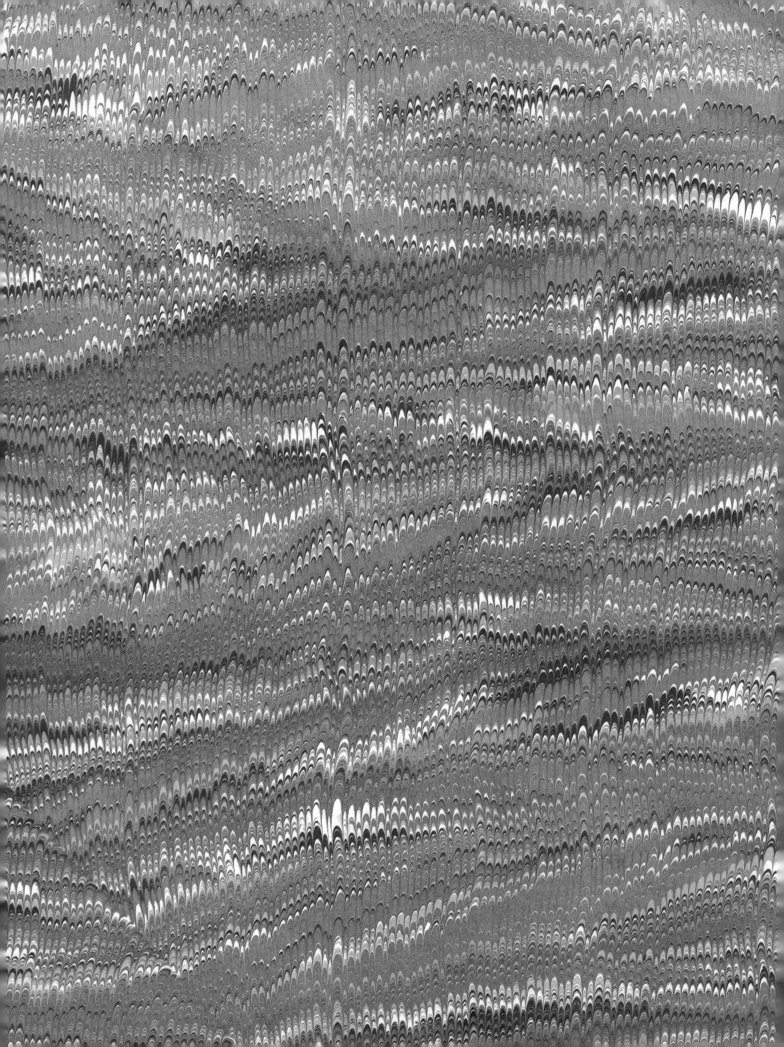